THE 20TH CENTURY IN CARTOONS

THE 20TH CENTURY IN CARTOONS

A history in pictures

ARCTURUS

ARCTURUS

This edition published in 2014 by Arcturus Publishing Limited
26/27 Bickels Yard, 151–153 Bermondsey Street,
London SE1 3HA

Picture Research and Caption Text:
Frances Evans

ISBN: 978-1-78404-433-6
AD004345UK

Printed in Malaysia

Contents

Primate

Neanderthal Man

Socrates

W. J. Bryan

INTRODUCTION

If you want to know what went on during the 20th century, if you want to meet the characters that defined it – the good, the bad and the ugly – or if you want to know about the big events that changed and shaped lives, countries and even entire continents, most of the key moments are here in this book. Some of them even took place in outer space.

The beauty of this book is that you don't need to buy a heavy tome with three thousand pages of words or spend hours surfing the internet, because the whole century is summed up in these pages through the eyes of the quick-witted masters of the pen and brush.

The cartoonist's gift is to simplify. Their job is to take the most complicated and sometimes controversial subjects and, with a few well-chosen strokes of the pen, plus a short caption, give you the full story.

'On with the Dance' by Pete Llanuza: Theodore Roosevelt is shown waltzing with anarchist William Schrenk, who shot the former president at close range during a campaign speech in Milwaukee on 2 October 1912. Roosevelt suffered a minor wound but went on to finish his speech.

'The Editorial Staff of *Krokodil*' (1929) by P. Belyanin: a Russian cartoonist sends up his work colleagues. Each one is lovingly characterized, including the little fellow on the table who is labelled 'the struggle against alcohol'.

Rather like the TV news correspondent who analyzes a difficult subject and filters it down to the bare essentials, cartoons are all about economy. They're also about finding the right angle.

Cartoonists come in every shape and size, with their own particular quirks and obsessions. They often used to be the stars of the newspapers they worked on and commanded the highest salaries.

Some had their fingers in many pies. For instance, Rube Goldberg, whose work from 1948 adorns the cover of this book, was an inventor, sculptor, author and engineer. Like Heath Robinson, his name is a byword for crazy, complicated contraptions which perform ridiculously simple tasks. He also produced political cartoons. During World War II he received so many death threats for denouncing Nazi Germany that his children had to change their surname for safety's sake.

Welsh cartoonist Leslie Illingworth took hours and hours to do each illustration. He didn't usually come up with ideas for his own work, relying on those close to him to supply topics. But few could compete when it came to producing painstakingly detailed drawings of historic events. An Illingworth cartoon is something to savour and never forget.

Washington Post cartoonist Herb Block was a crusader for truth, justice and the American way, which meant that he considered it his

THE NEW RELIGION

Estonia-born Ed Valtman was perhaps the only major US cartoonist of the Cold War era to experience Soviet rule. He emigrated to New Jersey in 1949. At a time when many in the West were mesmerized by Mao Zedong, 'The New Religion' (1966) shows a huge, Buddha-like figure borne aloft by brainwashed followers mindlessly chanting words from his *Little Red Book*. Valtman knew what lay behind the cult of personality.

TOP MAN — OR ELSE!

HOFFA'S ARROGANCE

U.S. PATIENCE

SHOEMAKER

Jimmy Hoffa was re-elected President of the International Brotherhood of Teamsters in 1961 despite accusations of racketeering from the US government. To rub salt in Washington's wounds, his salary was tripled – N.B. the muddy footprints up Uncle Sam's jacket in this cartoon by Vaughn Shoemaker. In 1964, Hoffa was jailed for jury tampering and other offences, and vanished off the face of the Earth in 1975. His body has never been found.

duty to beat up every incumbent of the White House during his five decades on the paper. But it was Senator Joseph McCarthy who had the thinnest skin. It's said he shaved twice a day to avoid being identified with the character that kept showing up in Herb Block's work with permanent five o'clock shadow.

New Zealand-born David Low made Adolf Hitler one of his favourite punchballs and after the war his name was found in Adolf's little black book – on the list of those to be executed once the Nazis had conquered Britain.

Cartoonists tend to have a strong sense of duty about skewering the pompous and duplicitous, the power-mad and the hypocritical on the end of their sharpest

nib. They love nothing more than cutting bloated personalities down to size, but some of their victims keep coming back for more. It's astonishing how many ask for original drawings 'to hang on the toilet wall'.

The process of how cartoonists work has hardly changed over the last 100 years. Cartoonists are first briefed by their editors. After studying the context of the story and the build-up to events, they will then go to their desk. They begin to draw some rough drafts, a few quick sketches, as ideas whir through their minds and they start to see the angle they'll take. On their return to the office, there's likely to be a bit of toing and froing, some editorial finessing, before the idea is agreed on. Once

'Satan Leads the Ball' (1942) by Arthur Syzk: born in Lodz, Poland, Szyk escaped to the US in 1940 and made art to fight the Nazis. Eleanor Roosevelt called him a 'one-man army'. He rejected modernism but still produced rich and detailed pictures such as this one, in which the devil, holding a Wagner score, leads the Axis gang – Hitler, Mussolini, Hirohito, Goebbels and Goering fit perfectly into the throng of grotesque stereotypes.

this is settled, it usually doesn't take long before the finished product materializes, for ever defining a moment in time.

The skill of cartoonists is as much about what they leave out as what they put in. The aim is to get the message across quickly, to make the point as sharp and profound as possible. There must be no confusion or ambiguity in what appears in print. You take one look at the cartoon and instantly get the message.

As a cartoonist it can be rewarding to know you've made a connection with the public. It's amusing to watch people on trains or buses reading their newspaper or iPad, seeing a grin appear as they spot the day's cutting cartoon. You notice them show their fellow passenger who nods and smiles in agreement. They share the joke – another cartoon that's hit the mark, lampooning some ludicrous public figure, speaking for and to everyone.

The cartoons here are also a fascinating

point of reference for changing styles, fashions and tastes over 100 years. They show that, while life moves on, many prejudices and attitudes don't move an inch. There are a few ancient certainties, though, that cartoonists rely on: mankind's lust for power and thirst for self-destruction. The cartoons here demonstrate that we are not very good at learning from our experiences; we endlessly repeat our mistakes. A cartoon from World War II could just as easily come from World War I, only the names and uniforms have changed. Greed and stupidity remain remarkably constant.

As you'll see, cartoonists are very good at chronicling misery – it's the source of much humour. But, paradoxically, what they make of it does much to cheer people up. The best cartoons enlighten, entertain and make you laugh in a way that often stays embedded in your mind.

This is an amazing record of a turbulent, fast-moving hundred years. The cartoonists keep pace with it, and in many cases are ahead of the game, predicting and warning us that the roads we sometimes take are ones we shouldn't go down. But hopefully, when you close the book at the end, you will be wiser as to what really went on in the 20th century.

Tony Husband

Press baron William Randolph Hearst, the model for Orson Welles' Citizen Kane, ran for Governor of New York in 1906 supported vociferously by his own editors. Rival magazine *Harper's Weekly* drew Hearst as the Straw Man in 'The Wizard of Ooze'.

1900s

It was all happening at the start of the century as the old made way for the new. Queen Victoria died, President McKinley was assassinated and the first Russian Revolution took place. Henry Ford produced the first affordable car, the Wright Brothers made the first manned flight and the US took over the building of the Panama Canal. In cities, populations exploded, demands for improved living conditions escalated and immigration to America went wild. Inventions included windscreen wipers, the Brownie camera, the Nickelodeon cinema and Plasticine. To top it all, ping-pong, the cheap and cheerful cousin of tennis invented by the British, winged its way around the world.

'The rare, the rather awful visits of Albert Edward, Prince of Wales, to Windsor Castle' (1921) by Max Beerbohm: Queen Victoria died on 22 January 1901, leaving her throne to her son Edward, who had spent 59 years as heir apparent, angering her with his drinking, gambling and numerous mistresses. Edward was Beerbohm's favourite subject for 'affectionate ridicule'; he continued to draw the king after his death in 1910.

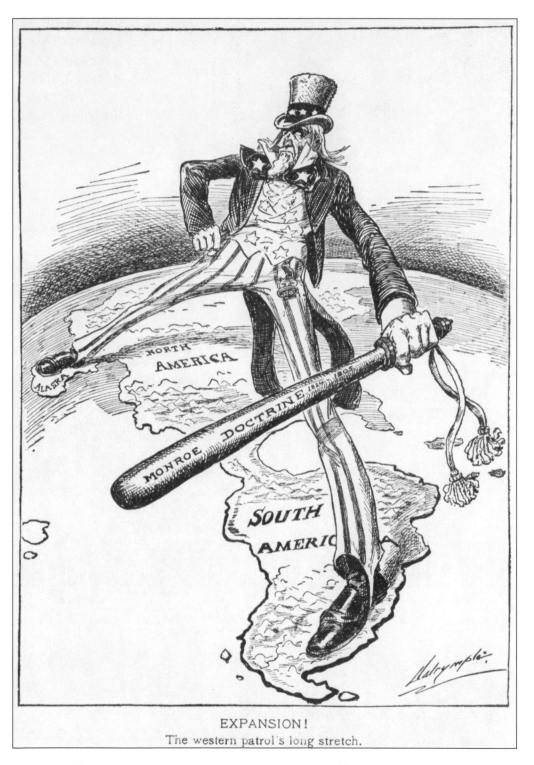

EXPANSION!
The western patrol's long stretch.

At the beginning of the century, America was emerging as a major world power. This cartoon from 1900 by Louis Dalrymple celebrates the Monroe Doctrine, a long-standing policy that excluded European countries from having interests in North or South America. The sketch is aimed squarely at the British (whose Navy enforced the doctrine in its early years), mimicking an earlier cartoon that showed the British Empire astride Africa.

LEFT: The New York subway first opened in 1904 and this cartoon, complaining of lousy service, was a riposte to an ad in *The World* which proclaimed, 'Harlem in 15 minutes'. Back then, it cost a nickel for a ride with the Interborough Rapid Transit, and the beadle-like figure on the platform is Father Knick, symbol of the city.

OPPOSITE: 'Liberty?' (1903) by John S. Pughe: immigrants arriving in the Land of the Free find a new statue – of a walking delegate of the unions – on the famous plinth overlooking New York harbour.

Frederick Burr Opper was a staff artist at Hearst newspapers in 1902. The cartoon above left was part of Hearst's campaign against the Trusts (large business corporations) and it shows one of Opper's invented stock characters, Mr Common Man, receiving a shock. Above right, John Bull has nearly the same leering face as the man from the Trust, with Opper suggesting that smoking too much opium in China led to Britain's delusions about the Boer War.

Above: Lord Kitchener leads his officers in a *danse macabre* around Britannia as they trample down the bodies of the Boer War dead in this French cartoon of 1902. Britain was criticized across Europe for its atrocities in South Africa.

Left: 'A Troublesome Egg to Hatch' (1901) by John S. Pughe: watched by the US and Japan, a weird set of chickens (the European powers) wait to see what they can get out of China.

The Nizam of Hyderabad and other notabilities playing "The Heavy Lead" in the Grand Spectacle entitled "The Delhi Durbar."

The Delhi Durbar was a mass assembly of Indian nobility, summoned to show allegiance to incoming British monarchs. It happened three times – in 1877, 1903 and 1911. In 1903, at the height of the British Empire, it was held to crown Edward VII and Queen Alexandra as Emperor and Empress of India. Everybody dressed up – as you can see from this drawing by E. T. Reed – and no expense was spared. A temporary light railway was built to reach the plain near Delhi where the event was taking place, there were gold candelabras on the elephants of the maharajahs, the police force was given its own special uniform and a glittering time was had by all. It's said that no greater collection of jewels has ever been assembled in one place. The celebrations lasted two weeks, but sadly Edward VII never turned up, sending his brother, The Duke of Connaught, instead.

THE MAN WHO CAN MAKE THE DIRT FLY.

French attempts to build the Panama Canal foundered on torrential rain, infernal heat, insects, snakes, swamps, yellow fever, malaria and bad planning: 20,000 men died. When the Americans took over in 1904, Roosevelt's administration cleared away the hangers-on (see drawing above by Louis Dalrymple), eradicated yellow fever and, by the time it opened in 1914, the 48-mile canal was a triumph of engineering linking the Atlantic to the Pacific.

H. T. Webster satirizes Theodore Roosevelt's insistence on regulating the railroads on such matters as charging the same rates to both large and small shippers for carrying the same products the same distance. Such intervention marked a sea change in American thought. Roosevelt wanted a 'Square Deal' for all parties, from which everyone would benefit.

One of the first major conflicts of the 20th century, the Russo-Japanese War (1904-5) saw Russia suffer embarrassing defeats at the hands of the Japanese Navy. Japan emerged as a modern, international power, referenced here by the victorious Samurai displaying the head of the Russian bear. The war was deeply unpopular in Russia and the rebellions that occurred in response planted the seeds for the revolution of 1917.

'Great Activity in Wall Street' (c.1908) by W. A. Rogers: the artist drily notes the cyclical nature of the markets – with ever-circling bulls, bears and lambs to the slaughter – as well as alluding to the unproductive nature of what they do.

The emphasis is on class in this pencil and Indian ink drawing by Englishman David Wilson (1905). The Lord Chancellor receives a brewer, a mine owner and a member of the Church, accommodating all of their requirements. However, despite the modesty of his request to ride along by the river, the working man is kicked straight out of the door.

LE TROISIÈME LARRON.

'The Third Thief' (1905), French: when Germany supported Morocco in seeking independence from France, Britain stepped in on the side of its Gallic neighbours, leading to the Entente Cordiale. Morocco is represented as a mouse, which Edward VII, Kaiser Wilhelm and Theophile Delcassé, the French Foreign Minister, all want to eat. This was a case of European nations fighting for control over the remnants of the Ottoman Empire.

GOOD-NATURED CARICATURES.   59

WILBUR WRIGHT.

Inspired by the Glider King, Otto Lilienthal, former bicycle mechanic Wilbur Wright teamed up with his brother Orville for the first heavier-than-air, manned, powered flight in 1903. The brothers continued to innovate and in 1909 Wilbur stunned a crowd of over 1,000,000 Americans into awed silence when he flew around the Statue of Liberty and followed the Hudson to Grant's Tomb.

This all-singing, all-dancing cartoon shows the huge number of political issues facing Ireland in 1905 – from the purity of beer and old age pensions to the vexed question of destitute aliens – but seems to suggest that Home Rule is the one the Irish keep parading round the show ring. The artist, a Unionist called Harrie Furniss, was born in Ireland and moved to England in 1876. He lived a colourful life and was once punched by Irish MP Swift MacNeill whom he had depicted as a gorilla. In 1914, he produced one of the first animated cartoons for Thomas Edison in the US.

Tsar Nicholas II is astonished to discover how the ordinary Russian has grown in the last year in this offering from French magazine *L'Assiette au Beurre* from 1906. Nicholas survived the Russian Revolution of 1905 which followed the nation's defeat in the Russo-Japanese war. But he continued to be high-handed in dealing with the problems of his impoverished country and he and his family paid the price when they were executed in 1918.

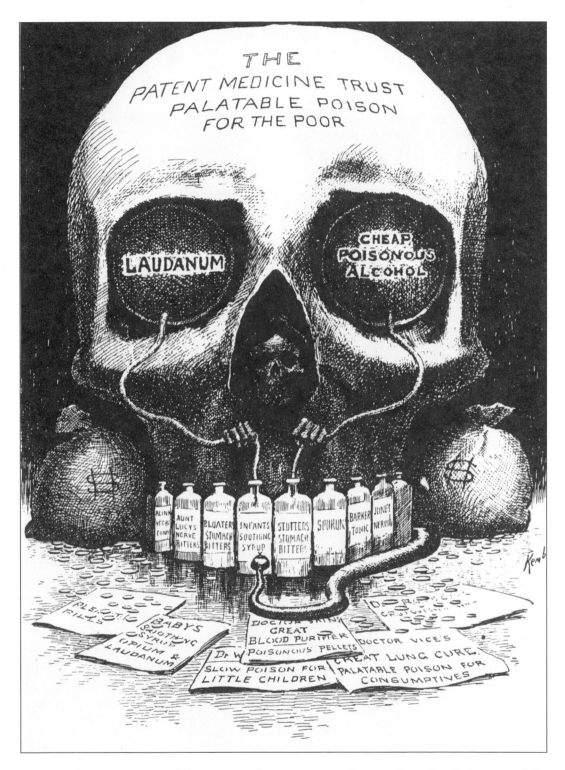

Patent medicines were a scandal in 1906. In the US, Mrs. Winslow's Soothing Cough Syrup was full of opium and mothers used it to send their babies to sleep – they didn't always wake up. As a New York drugstore proprietor put it, 'People ask what catarrh remedies we got and pick the one with the most cocaine. When I see a customer comparing the labels, I know she's a fiend.' (by E. W. Kemble)

A chauffeur speeds through a city street amid a swirl of headlines about the dangers of motoring, leaving plumes of dust in his wake. In the early part of the century there was panic over the arrival of cars on the roads, even though the death toll in horse-related accidents was 3,850 times higher. In the 1890s, a 'horseless carriage' had to be preceded by a pedestrian with a red flag or lantern (to warn of its approach), but now the brakes were off. The speed limit was set at 20 mph in most US states and a Ford Model T retailed at $950. This was to be the century of the car.

'Une table à Monaco' by Georges Goursat (aka 'Sem'), published in Le Rire in 1900: Goursat was a well-known caricaturist of France's 'Belle Epoque' (1870s–1914). Here he presents figures from some of Europe's financial dynasties – the Rothschilds and Oppenheims – accompanied by French actress Polaire and courtesan Emilienne d'Alençon, enjoying the high-life in Monte Carlo.

'The Weaker Sex?' (1903): fashionable illustrator Charles Dana Gibson set the standards for female beauty with his 'Gibson Girls'. They were often dutiful and passive, but here he turns the world he created on its head – one of his gorgeous creations prepares to poke a tiny man with her hatpin as if he were an entomological specimen.

LEFT: 'Before the Trojan Horse is Admitted the Puzzled Citizen Will Be Shown a Little More Fully' (1909): a puzzled citizen of Missouri scratches his head at the creature before him – an octopus representing Standard Oil disguised as a horse.

SUFFRAGETTES AT HOME.

He. "I SAY, THAT LADY OVER THERE LOOKS RATHER OUT OF IT."
She. "YES, YOU SEE, MOST OF US HERE HAVE BEEN IN PRISON TWO OR THREE TIMES, AND SHE, POOR DEAR, HAS ONLY BEEN BOUND OVER!"

WHO 'LL BELL THE CAT?

TOP: A joke about the gentility of leading suffragettes and the badge of honour that came with being jailed for the cause. Drawing by Arthur Wallis Mills, 1909.

RIGHT: Nobel Prize-winners, Polish-born Marie Curie and her French husband Pierre, in a cartoon from *Vanity Fair*, 1904, which rather unfairly shows him as the leading light. In 1898, they discovered the elements polonium and radium. To this day, Marie's notebooks are still too radioactive to touch.

LEFT: Despotic House Speaker Joseph G. Cannon, depicted by Clifford Berryman as a cat. Republican rebel mice draw lots to see who will put the bell on the cat's collar to warn he is on his way.

A disreputable chorus backs an anti-suffrage soprano in this cartoon from *Puck*, published on 9 October 1915. Pro-suffrage campaigners argued that female voters would support laws against prostitution, child labour and other social ills.

1910s

The 1910s were dominated by World War I, which began on 4 August 1914. When an armistice was agreed on 11 November 1918, over 16 million people had lost their lives and Europe had changed beyond all recognition. Revolutions also broke out across the globe, such as the Chinese Revolution of 1911 and the Russian Revolution of 1917. Western nations saw struggles for improved working conditions and women's rights. Scott's doomed expedition to the South Pole in 1912 and the sinking of the RMS *Titanic* the same year haunted the popular imagination for decades to come. By 1919, the generation that had survived the Great War was ready to lose itself in the 'Roaring Twenties'.

THE START FOR THE POLE.

The Antarctics. "GREAT SCOTT, THEY'RE OFF!"

[The *Terra Nova* is announced to sail from London on the South Polar Expedition on June 1.]

By the 1910s, Antarctica was the last unexplored continent and wealthy nations were racing to claim the prize of the South Pole. Leonard Raven-Hill's cartoon from *Punch* captures the optimistic mood that accompanied Robert Falcon Scott's British team as they left Cardiff on 15 June 1910. In the end, Roald Amundsen's Norwegian party got there first. Tragically, Scott and four companions perished on the return journey.

Australian cartoonist Will Dyson was well known for his socialist views. Here Dyson uses the 'Ape-like-Man controversy' to pose a social critique – what right does anyone have to put other creatures in cages, whether these involve literal bars or invisible class barriers? The contrast between the rigid, well-dressed human observers and the mother and baby monkey, presented in a Madonna-and-child-like pose, questions what 'humanity' means.

INSPECTOR OF BUILDINGS!

RECORD FIRE
FOR NEW YORK
145
LIVES LOST!!!!
BUILDING FIRE PROOF
ONLY FIRE ESCAPE
COLLAPSED.
OUR INSPECTOR

These two cartoons respond to the Triangle Shirtwaist Factory Fire which broke out on 25 March 1911 and was one of the worst disasters to occur in New York City until the September 11 attacks in 2001. 145 workers died in the fire. Many of the victims were young women from Jewish or Italian immigrant communities who were unable to escape from the building because the doors had been locked to stop them taking unauthorized breaks. The tragedy led to improved safety standards in factories and brought about the rise of the International Ladies' Garment Workers' Union, which became a major voice in the American labour movement during the 1920s and 1930s.

ORIGINAL CAPTION: *The Editor of the 'Daily Herald', having been summoned before the Marconi Select Committee, has an awful vision of himself in a like position before the Inner Council of Ten of Capitalism, as figured by the fevered imagination of our Cartoonist.*

The Marconi Scandal broke in the summer of 1912. Several high-profile MPs were accused of profiting from information about the British government's relation with the Marconi Company, a telecommuncations pioneer. Will Dyson's cartoon exposes the relationship between government and big businesses, as well as expressing anxieties about press freedoms.

A golden calf has displaced the Statue of Liberty in this cartoon attacking greed from 1912. The relationship between government and big business was a hot topic during the presidential election that year, the outcome of which depended on the working-class vote. In September, the Democratic candidate (and eventual winner) Woodrow Wilson delivered a campaign speech calling for the end of business monopolies.

THE BOILING POINT.

By 1912 the gradual erosion of the Ottoman Empire had left a power vacuum, which other European countries were jostling to fill. This cartoon by Leonard Raven-Hill, featured in *Punch* on 2 October 1912, captures the precarious situation. Britain, Germany, France, Russia and Austria-Hungary nervously balance on top of a boiling pot of 'Balkan Troubles'. The Balkan Wars began six days after the cartoon was published.

TOLL OF THE SEA.

[Dedicated to the memory of the brave men who went down in the *Titanic*, April 15th.]

Tears for the dead, who shall not come again
 Homeward to any shore on any tide!
Tears for the dead! but through that bitter rain
 Breaks, like an April sun, the smile of pride.

What courage yielded place to others' need,
 Patient of discipline's supreme decree,
Well may we guess who know that gallant breed
 Schooled in the ancient chivalry of the sea! O. S.

On the morning of the 15 April 1912, the RMS *Titanic* struck an iceberg in the North Atlantic and sank, taking with it the lives of more than 1,500 passengers and crew. Bernard Partridge's response to the disaster was published in *Punch* on 24 April and shows Britannia and Liberty united in grief. Partridge also contributed to the souvenir programme for the Dramatic and Operatic Matinee held at Covent Garden in aid of the Titanic Disaster Fund in May 1912.

"'A Little Child Shall Feed Them": Biblical Law as Interpreted by Employers of Child-Labor' by Art Young appeared in *Life* magazine in February 1911. By the 1910s American labour reform movements were growing and with them increasing challenges to the use of child workers. A year after this cartoon was printed Congress established the US Children's Bureau, which became instrumental in discouraging child labour.

ABOVE: A newspaper editor and proprietor is presented as a prostitute, selling himself to a fat cat who, as the list on his trousers confirms, owns just about every other business out there, from breakfast food companies and breweries to railroads and banks. Art Young produced this cartoon for left-wing magazine *The Masses* in 1912.

RIGHT: Sigmund Freud, the founding father of psychoanalysis, analyzing himself. In 1910 Freud had formally established the International Psychoanalytical Association, the world's first regulatory body for psychoanalysis. Ten years earlier, Freud's *Interpretation of Dreams* had introduced his theory of the unconscious to the world.

THE HOME RULE MAZE.

Mr. Asquith. "EXCUSE ME, SIR, BUT ARE YOU TRYING TO GET IN OR OUT?"
Mr. Bonar Law. "JUST WHAT I WAS GOING TO ASK *YOU*, SIR."

The Third Home Rule Bill (1914) was supposed to allow Ireland to become a self-governing entity within the United Kingdom. Herbert Henry Asquith was a supporter of the bill; Andrew Bonar Law was opposed to it. As Leonard Raven-Hill's cartoon for *Punch* suggests, however, quite what either minister wants to achieve in Ireland is easily lost in the maze of Home Rule politics.

Les Hommes du Jour

Annales Politiques. Sociales. Littéraires et Artistiques

LA PREMIERE ET LA PLUS INOUBLIA BLE VICTIME DE LA GUERRE   Directeur : HENRI FABRE.

lucien laforge

(Dessin de Lucien Laforge)

Hebdomadaire : le Samedi

JAURÈS... malgré eux !

25 CENTIMES

Jean Jaurès was a founding member of the French Socialist Party and an anti-militarist. In the weeks leading up to war, Jaurès made enemies by calling for a reconcilliation between Germany and France and, on 31 July 1914, he was assassinated by a French nationalist. *Les Hommes du Jour* was a left-leaning publication and its regular artist, Lucien Laforge, presents Jaurès as the protector of French liberty 'despite them' (*malgré eux!*).

ONLY THE NAVY CAN STOP THIS

This US Navy poster incorporates a cartoon by W. A. Rogers, showing Germany wading through a sea of dead bodies. Attacks on civilian ships, such as the RMS *Lusitania* (which was also carrying arms), influenced the US government's decision to join the conflict in 1917. The *Lusitania* was hit by a German torpedo on 7 May 1915. Most of the 1,198 who lost their lives were British or Canadian, but 128 Americans were also among the dead.

UNCONQUERABLE

THE KAISER: "So, you see—you've lost everything."
THE KING OF THE BELGIANS: "Not my soul."

By Bernard Partridge, published in *Punch* on 21 October 1914. That summer King Albert I had refused Kaiser Wilhelm's request to move German soldiers through neutral Belgium in order to attack France. When German forces invaded Belgium, Albert's army held back the Kaiser's troops to allow Britain and France time to prepare for the First Battle of the Marne (5–12 September 1914) which resulted in an Allied victory.

THE HARVEST MOON

(Aug. 31, 1914)

ABOVE: This cartoon by American artist Luther D. Bradley was published shortly after the outbreak of war and predicts the devastating human cost of the conflict. By the time the war ended on 11 November 1918 over 10,000,000 soldiers had died, two-thirds of these on the battlefields.

RIGHT: Australia greeted the outbreak of war with enthusiasm. From a population of fewer than 5 million, 416,809 Australian men enlisted and Prime Minister Andrew Fisher declared that the country would support Britain to 'the last man and the last shilling'. British soldiers peek out of Australia's protective pouch in this German cartoon, which suggests that the old colonial power was relying heavily on the support of the younger nation.

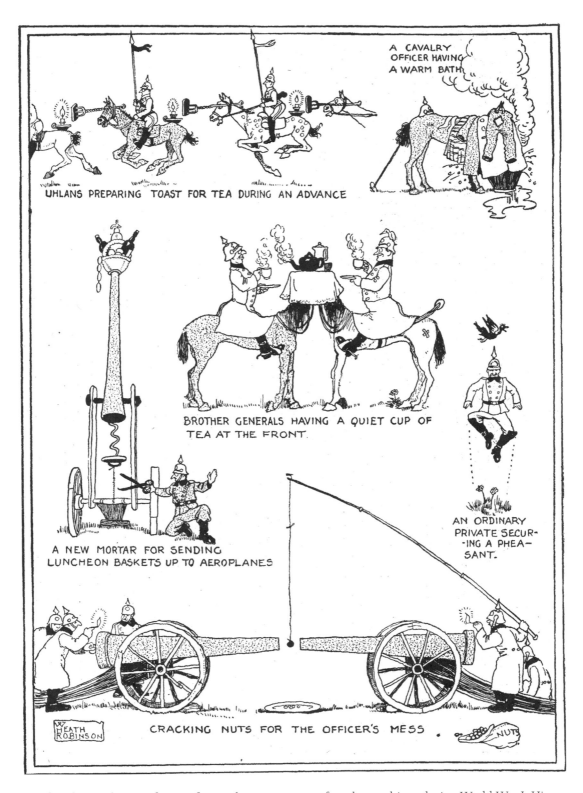

Heath Robinson became famous for producing cartoons of wacky machines during World War I. His name even became a byword during the war years for makeshift contraptions. Here Robinson suggests some fanciful ways members of the armed forces might prepare their tea and toast at the front.

'No More Fish': the British aristocracy respond to the death of Lord Kitchener by lamenting their culinary losses in this cartoon by Ragnvald Blix for German satirical magazine *Simplicissimus* (June 1916). A month earlier, Kitchener had been on a diplomatic mission to Russia when his ship, HMS *Hampshire*, struck a German mine and sank off the Orkney Islands.

THE WAR WORKERS.

"WHAT'S ALL THIS CACKLE ABOUT VOTES AND A NEW REGISTER?"
"DON'T KNOW—OR CARE. WE'RE ALL TOO BUSY JUST NOW."

As this cartoon from *Punch* reflects, the crisis of war sidelined calls for women's suffrage. With men leaving their jobs to fight, new employment opportunities became available for women. But the British government and press were keen to exaggerate the facts – in reality, the majority of male-dominated professions were still closed to female workers and their wages were significantly lower than those of their male counterparts.

ABOVE: Canadian-American artist Boardman Robinson was fiercely anti-militarist and witnessed the effects of the war first-hand when he travelled to Europe in 1915. Returning to America he produced several cartoons, including this one, for *The Masses*. When America joined the war in 1917 Robinson's work, combined with the magazine's socialist stance, attracted the attention of federal prosecutors and the publication was closed down.

'The Pacifist's Dream' by Clifford Berryman appeared in the *Washington Evening Star* on 31 March 1917, weeks before America entered the war. Here the pacifist ironically imagines how he might frustrate America's involvement in the conflict – by locking Uncle Sam in the stocks and treating him violently.

A puppet-like Tsar Nicholas II and Tsarina Alexandra perch on Grigori Rasputin's knees in a Russian cartoon that criticizes the latter's influence over the imperial court (the heading reads 'The Russian Tsars at Home…'). Printed in 1916, the image reflects the mounting hostility towards Rasputin, who many blamed for Russia's failures in the war. On 19 December, Rasputin's body was found in the frozen Neva River in St Petersburg.

Cartoon by T. E. Powers, International News Service, from "The Odyssey of Henry Ford and the Great Peace Ship"

In 1915 American industrialist Henry Ford organized an amateur peace mission to Europe and invited prominent pacifists to join him. Almost all of Ford's invitees declined, and the comic atmosphere that accompanied the departure of the 'Peace Ship' gave cartoonists ample material to work with. The squirrels visible in this cartoon by T. E. Powers were left on the gangplank before the *Oscar II* set sail, with a sign on their cage reading 'To the Good Ship Nutty'.

AMERICA TO THE FRONT.

[In view of the present needs of the Allies, America has not waited to complete the independent organisation of her Army, but has sent her troops forward to be brigaded with British and French units.]

In the face of submarine attacks and blockades on American ships President Wilson decided to call for 'a war to end all wars'. Congress voted to declare war on Germany on 6 April 1917. By June, 14,000 American troops were stationed in France; by May 1918 there were over 1,000,000 US troops fighting in Europe. Leonard Raven-Hill's cartoon greets their arrival as a welcome relief for exhausted Allied forces.

COPPER TRUST TO THE PRESS: "IT'S ALL RIGHT, PAL; JUST TELL THEM HE WAS A TRAITOR."

The Industrial Workers of the World (IWW) was founded in 1905 to protect the interests of working people. Frank Little had joined in 1906 and became a prominent union leader. In July 1917 he travelled to Butte, Montana to head a miners' strike against the Anaconda Copper Company, one of the largest trusts in America at the time. He was attacked in the early hours of 1 August, beaten and lynched from a railway trestle. This IWW cartoon exposes attempts by the Copper Trust and the press to cover up the story.

An anti-communist cartoon by W. A. Rogers published at the height of the First Red Scare (1919–1921), which had been sparked by the events of the Bolshevik Revolution of 1917. Revolutionary leaders Lenin and Trotsky are presented as reptiles, cold-bloodedly observing as the Allies (Japan, Britain, America and Czechoslovakia) carry away the wounded Russian bear.

A full-bearded Bolshevik peers out from underneath the American flag,
threatening to set it alight with his torch of 'Anarchy' in this cartoon from
1919. That summer, fear that the workers' revolution in Russia could spread to
America was rife and a series of mail bombs, race riots and strikes only served
to fan the flames of hysteria and xenophobia.

The Family of Nations

The Liberator, August, 1919.

Soviet Russia

Boardman Robinson

ABOVE: This cartoon by Art Young featured in the January 1919 edition of left-wing magazine *The Liberator*, and comments on the relationships between global powers post-World War 1. *The Liberator* was formed as a successor to *The Masses* in 1918.

Boardman Robinson's rather crazy – almost touchingly naïve – sketch presents Russia as an entirely virtuous and vulnerable nation, surrounded by hostile forces. Robinson produced this cartoon for *The Liberator* in August 1919 at the height of the Russian Civil War.

Maurice Becker

Planning the Next War

This cartoon by Russian-born Maurice Becker also appeared in _The Liberator_ in August 1919. Foreign leaders
– in particular the United States – were anxious that the new post-revolutionary government in Mexico might
take a communist turn, following in the footsteps of Russia.

The League of Nations was formed in the aftermath of World War I to maintain world peace. President Wilson had been instrumental in setting up the organization, but America refused to join. Germany and Russia were deliberately excluded. Boardman Robinson's image of Death's hand signing the peace treaty anticipates the failure of the League, whose exclusionist policies helped set the stage for the events of World War II.

Die Grundlage für den Völkerbund

(Th. Th. Heine)

„Nur so kann Deutschland darin geduldet werden!"

This cartoon by Thomas Theodor Heine responds to the terms of the Treaty of Versailles, which were considered to be very harsh by most Germans, and appeared in the German magazine *Simplicissimus* in April 1919. British Prime Minister David Lloyd George, French Prime Minister Georges Clemenceau and US President Wilson are presented as avenging angels standing on a dead body representing Germany. The image was titled '*Nur so kann Deuschland darin geduldet werden*' ('The only way Germany can be tolerated').

Karl Arnold depicts the dance-epidemic in 1920s Germany. The Weimar Republic faced severe economic problems post-war, but this couldn't stop the jazz craze from sweeping through its cities. Dancer Josephine Baker visited Berlin in 1925 and recalled how the 'vast cafes reminded me of ocean liners powered by the rhythms of their orchestras'.

1920s

The 1920s was a decade of economic prosperity and cultural freedom in Europe and America. People flocked to the cities seeking new opportunities, bright young things kicked the night away to the Charleston and jazz tunes filled art-deco mansions in the ever-expanding Hollywood Hills. But a seedier side to these excesses occasionally showed through. Prohibition encouraged the rise of powerful mafia groups in America. Radical political movements also emerged from the turmoil of World War I – communist parties in Russia and China and fascist groups in Italy and Germany. When the Wall Street Crash began in 1929, the decade-long party was well and truly over.

The Woman Patriot was published between 1918 and 1932, billed as a 'defense AGAINST Suffragism, feminism and Socialism'. This edition responds to the passing of the Nineteenth Amendment in August 1920, which stopped any American citizen from being denied the right to vote on the basis of gender.

"TWO'S COMPANY, THREE'S A CROWD."
—Chapin in the St. Louis *Republic*.

A suffragette sits between the Democrat donkey and the Republican elephant in this cartoon from June 1919, implying that both parties wanted to keep women's votes for themselves.

Australian Bert Hinkler made the first solo flight between Britain and Australia in 1928, departing from Croydon on 7 February and arriving in Darwin on 22 February. He reduced the England-Australia record from 28 to 15½ days.

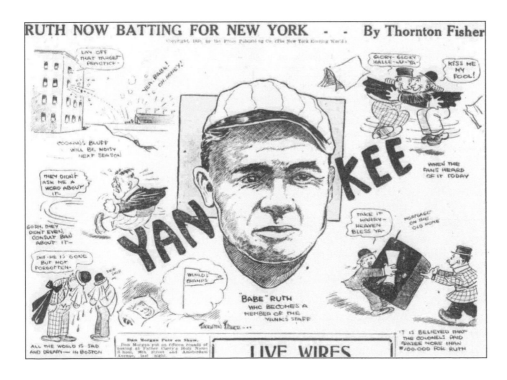

On 6 January 1920 Harry Frazee, owner of the Boston Red Sox, sold star baseball player Babe Ruth to the New York Yankees for $100,000. Frazee was also a theatre producer and reputedly needed the cash to fund a musical, *No, No, Nanette*.

New Masses

Governor Fuller: "Cheer up, Judge, it will soon be over."

Above: Art Young depicts an anxious Judge Webster Thayer who sentenced Italian-born anarchists Nicola Sacco and Bartolomeo Vanzetti to death for murder in 1927, despite fears the evidence was fixed. Their appeals gained support from the likes of Albert Einstein and H. G. Wells, but Governor Fuller refused to grant clemency.
Opposite: Dorothy Parker (text) and Anne Harriet Fish (cartoons) target America's rising divorce rates (1920).

THE RENO SPECIAL

Any time that you want to see a bit of life, go to the nearest railroad station and watch the outgoing trains to Nevada. Several ticket agents have to be constantly on duty in the window where round-trip tickets to Reno are sold; one man couldn't keep up with the rush of trade. A typical line at the ticket office is shown here—it is considered *de rigeur* for husbands to accompany their outgoing wives to the train. If you are contemplating any little jaunt to the nation's reconstruction center in the near future, it is safer to get seats several weeks ahead. Traffic over these lines grows heavier every season

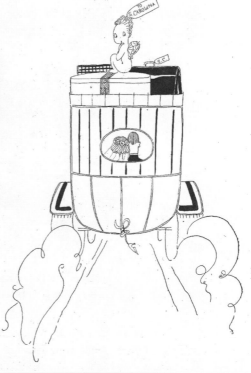

OLD HOME WEEK

It is so nice for the new bridegroom to meet his wife's collection of former husbands. It is something for him to look forward to, all through the honeymoon. These little family gatherings are so delightfully homey—it is always reassuring to feel that you are all members of the same club. Men who thoughtlessly marry a hitherto unmarried girl do miss so much in life; they never have the chance to meet their brother heroes, and to while away an hour exchanging experiences

BACK TO THE START

This little scene is the sort of thing that divorce leads to,—hope springs eternal, and all that. A divorce simply gets one into the right frame of mind for a fresh start in matrimony. After all, Nature will have its own way; there's nothing like love—it is what the divorce lawyers and Reno hotel keepers attribute all their success to

THIS is Mr. Bernard Shaw,
Who has got a gifted jaw ;
Though it 's hid by hairy fluff
You can hear it fast enough.

When they praise his lofty brow,
Saying, "Where is Shakespeare now ?"
Modestly he says, "O fie !
Shakespeare 's quite as good as I."

When he talks to eager youth,
Letting fall some grains of truth,
He will choke them up with chaff,
Loth to go without a laugh.

Some may think it wrong to rank
Bernard as a mountebank ;
Others find it just as odd
To regard him as a god.

MR. PUNCH'S PERSONALITIES.
I.—MR. GEORGE BERNARD SHAW.

Bernard Partridge produced this portrait of playwright George Bernard Shaw for *Punch* in 1925, the year Shaw received a Nobel Prize in Literature. Shaw remains the only person to have been awarded both a Nobel Prize in Literature and an Oscar (in 1938 for the film adaptation of *Pygmalion*).

ALL THINGS TO ALL RANKS.

How to dance with—

A Subaltern.

A Captain.

A Major.

And a Colonel.

This 1925 *Punch* cartoon characterizes ranks of the British Army through their nimble footwork. The Captain seems to favour the Tango while the Major is more of a Swing-man. Many famous dancers and choreographers – such as Fred Astaire and Busby Berkeley – began their careers in the 1920s.

SOUNDS ACROSS THE SEA.

JONATHAN (*on the new wireless telephone*). "THANKS, JOHN. SOME EARFUL."

In January 1923 the first wireless telephone call was made between New York and London. In an address to the American Telephone and Telegraph Company later that year, the organization's vice president J. J. Carty recalled how the 'talking was continued for two hours, and the voices of all the speakers at New York were plainly heard in London [...] everything they said was as plainly heard as you are now hearing me.'

MR. PUNCH "PRESENTS" A FEW SCREEN OPPORTUNITIES FOR PROMINENT ASPIRANTS.

Bernard Partridge's vignettes for *Punch* (1922) give a snapshot of the political scene via films of the day. Characters include Irish politician Eamon de Valera, prohibition advocate William E. 'Pussyfoot' Johnson, newspaper baron Lord Northcliffe and ex-First Lord of the Admiralty Eric Geddes. The pairing of artist Augustus John with *The Headless Man* refers to an incident when Lord Leverhulme returned his portrait to John minus its head. This slur on John's artistic integrity prompted a 24-hour strike by artists in Paris and a march through Hyde Park, where students burnt a headless effigy of Leverhulme.

The 1918 influenza (or 'Spanish Flu') pandemic lasted for two years and was one of the deadliest natural disasters in human history. Around 500 million people were infected, and 50 to 100 million of these died as a result of the flu. This 1923 cartoon by Dana Gibson was commissioned by the Rockefeller Institute of Medical Research (New York) to remind the public about the dangers of the disease.

OPPOSITE: 'If This Thing Grows Much Bigger I May Have to Drop It'. In 1922 it was revealed that Albert B. Fall, US Secretary of the Interior, had leased federal oil reserves to companies in return for cash. One of these reserves was in Wyoming and covered in a teapot-shaped rock, which the monster in this 1924 cartoon by John Conacher personifies. Fall received a prison sentence in 1931 for his role in the 'Teapot Dome Scandal'.

Calvin Coolidge succeeded Warren G. Harding as US President in 1923. Under Coolidge, America experienced a period of rapid economic growth, but not everyone agreed with his view that 'Business [was] America's business'. D. R. Fitzpatrick, editorial cartoonist for the *St. Louis Dispatch* and two-time Pulitzer Prize Winner, underlines the popularity of Coolidge's laissez-faire policies with business leaders in this cartoon from 1924.

This Italian cartoon from 1925 highlights the widespread manipulation of the press by Benito Mussolini's National Fascist Party. Figures resembling Hitler and Stalin survey the latest Italian news developments. One of the newspaper's pasted on the wall, *Il Popolo d'Italia* ('The People of Italy'), had been founded by Mussolini in 1914 and became a platform for his fascist party following World War I.

Winsor McCay was a prominent American editorial cartoonist and an early pioneer of animation. He was particularly noted for his use of linear perspective, which is showcased in this bold cityscape that was probably created for the *New York American* newspaper in the early 1920s. McCay highlights the uglier side to the 'Roaring Twenties' – bootleg alcohol, organized crime, drugs and fraudulent money-making (note how one high-rise building is practically exploding with ticker tape).

MANNERS AND MODES AT DEAUVILLE.

THE EXCLUSIVE BATHER.

DIGNITY AND IMPUDENCE.   COCKTAIL HOUR ON THE PLAGE.

Lewis Baumer captures high society at play at Deauville, on France's Normandy coast (*Punch*, 1927). The town's popularity exploded in the 1920s, when its casino, grand hotels and racetrack made the resort the destination of choice for the international upper classes. In F. Scott Fitzgerald's *The Great Gatsby* (1925), Daisy and Tom Buchanan visit the town on their honeymoon.

Primate — **Neanderthal Man** — **Socrates** — **W. J. Bryan**

ABOVE: In 1925 high school teacher John Scopes found himself on trial, accused of violating Tennessee's 'Butler Act', under which it was illegal to teach evolution. Scopes was defended by Clarence Darrow and the prosecution was represented by William Jennings Bryan. This pro-evolution cartoon by Rea Irvin for *The New Yorker* depicts the 'Rise and Fall of Man', with Bryan representing a regression towards Neanderthal-thinking.

LEFT: Heath Robinson offers a typically whimsical reflection on the development of aviation during World War I in 'Humours of Flying', which was included in a book called *The Illustrated War Record of the Most Notable Episodes in the Great European War 1914–1918* (c. 1920).

SYRACUSE HERALD: FRIDAY EVENING, JUNE 17, 1927.

GREETINGS FROM MARS

This cartoon of Charles A. Lindbergh by Syracusan Frank H. Ladendorf appeared in the old Syracuse Herald June 17, 1927.

Charles A. Lindbergh was a relative unknown when he made his historic non-stop solo flight from New York to Paris on 20–21 May 1927. Lindbergh became the first person in history to be in New York one day and Paris the next and was awarded the Medal of Honor for his achievement. Frank H. Ladendorf created this cartoon to commemorate Lindbergh's flight in June 1927.

CHICAGO COP: WHAT'VE YOU GOT IN THAT CAR?
GANGSTER: NOTHIN' BUT BOOZE, OFFICER.
COP: I BEG YOUR PARDON—I THOUGHT IT MIGHT BE HISTORY BOOKS.

This image from the Prohibition era wryly comments on political graft in American cities. The statue in the background features a self-congratulatory slayer of lions and old ladies called 'Hizzoner', urban slang for 'His Honor', and a reference to the corruption that allowed fortunes to be made out of illegal booze in the 1920s. It was widely felt that city mayors were turning a blind eye to everything that was going on under their noses.

THE SQUAWKIE.

Thespis (*to Cinema*). "GREAT HOLLYWOOD! IS THAT THING OUR CHILD?"

Warner Bros' *The Jazz Singer* was the first feature-length film to incorporate synchronized dialogue. Released on 6 October 1927 it became one of the biggest box-office hits of that year, ushering in the era of 'the talkies' and marking the decline of silent cinema. This Bernard Partridge cartoon, published in *Punch* in 1929, shows Thespis, the husband of Cinema, reacting with horror when presented with their noisy offspring.

BEWARE OF STOWAWAYS, MR. HOOVER!

Herbert Hoover won a landslide victory in the presidential election of 1928. Before his inauguration he made a ten-week tour of South America, promoting his plans to reduce American interference in Latin American affairs. This cartoon illustrates his departure on the battleship *Maryland*. The artist suggests that, even at sea, Hoover won't be able to escape from 'office-seekers' (people seeking appointment in the new administration).

TAIL HOLT

A desperate investor clings to the tail of the runaway 'Bear Market' in this prescient cartoon by
Rollin Kirby. The image was published in *The New York World* three weeks before the beginning
of the Wall Street Crash in late October 1929. The crash signalled the beginning of the Great
Depression, which affected all Western industrialized countries throughout the 1930s.

Bankrupt brokers line up to throw themselves out of the office window following the stock market crash. Rumours abounded of people committing suicide on Wall Street. It is difficult to verify the extent to which these were true – *Variety* magazine, for instance, reported at the time that the numbers were being suppressed from the papers. But the idea was certainly sustained by cartoons like this.

In the wake of the Great Depression, Franklin D. Roosevelt's government passed the 'New Deal', a series of laws focused on 'Relief, Recovery and Reform'. Herbert Johnson's cartoon from 1936 is sceptical about these policies: here the taxpayer is drawn into dangerous levels of debt by senseless spending.

1930s

The 1930s began with the world struggling to deal with the fall-out from the Wall Street Crash. Economic hardships enabled the rise of authoritarian regimes in Germany, Italy and Spain. Conflicts broke out elsewhere too – 1937 saw the start of the Second Sino-Japanese War, the largest Asian war of the 20th century. The decade was also marked by technological developments: radar was invented, Kodachrome created and nuclear fission discovered. Innovative films, such as the first full-length animation, Walt Disney's *Snow White and the Seven Dwarfs* (1937), provided welcome escapism for audiences as the world once again headed towards war. On 1 September 1939 World War II, the deadliest conflict in human history, began.

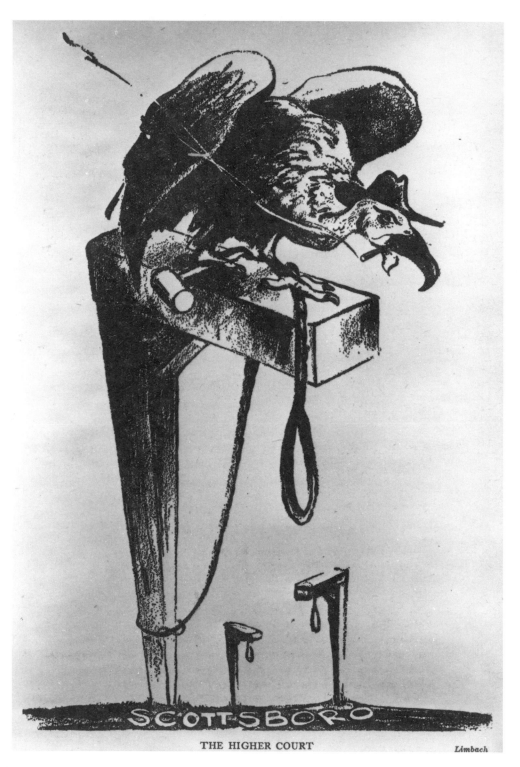

THE HIGHER COURT

Limbach

The Higher Court appears as a vulture ready to descend on the Scottsboro Boys, nine African-Americans charged with raping two white girls in Alabama in 1931. The case was influenced by racism and is now viewed as a miscarriage of justice. Eight of the boys were initially sentenced to death. After retrials four were pardoned and the rest forced to serve prison sentences. The case eventually led to the end of all-white juries in the South.

This cartoon from 1930 comments on the presence of criminal gangs in Chicago following the St Valentine's Day Massacre of 1929. Members of an Italian-American group led by gangster Al Capone had allegedly gunned down seven mobsters from a rival Irish gang. Capone's triumph was short-lived. In 1931 he was found guilty of tax evasion and sentenced to 11 years in jail, four of which were spent in the notorious Alcatraz prison.

'Come with me and we'll attend their jubilee / And see them spend their last two bits / Puttin' on the Ritz', so goes Irving Berlin's famous Depression-era song. But the clubland of post-Crash New York was a far cry from the glamorous heyday of the 1920s. In this cartoon by Charles Forbell, the few remaining club members huddle in the middle of a rubbish-strewn room, the excesses of the past having come back to haunt them.

LEFT: A homeless man reacts with disbelief to President Hoover's assessment of the state of the country during the elections of 1932. Hoover was widely blamed for the Depression – shanty towns constructed during this period were popularly known as 'Hoovervilles'. By 1932 over 13 million Americans had lost their jobs and 2 million were homeless.

BELOW: In this cartoon from 1931, Canadian artist Jimmy Frise highlights the issue of campaign finance reform. Four year later, the slogan 'On to Ottawa' was adopted by a union which was protesting against the notoriously poor conditions in work camps during the Depression.

Small wonder the candidate yields to temptation when Special Privilege rolls down on him and beckons with that come-hither look, old John B. Public meanwhile shooting by without so much as a look at the road-weary traveller.   Cartoon by FRISE

This *Punch* cartoon from 1932 celebrates the achievement of British nuclear physicist Norman Feather, who was the first to split the oxygen atom. Feather was a Fellow of Trinity College, Cambridge – hence the reference to the 'Good Old Light Blues!'.

Wife. "BUT, DARLING, WHATEVER IS IT? HAVE YOU WON THE CROSSWORD PRIZE?"
Scientist (old sport). "BETTER THAN THAT. GOOD OLD LIGHT BLUES! THEY'VE SPLIT ANOTHER ATOM!"
[With Mr. Punch's compliments to Mr. FEATHER, of Trinity College, Cambridge, who has disintegrated the oxygen nucleus for the first time.]

Clifford Berryman tackles Prohibition in 1932. The Democrats wanted to repeal Prohibition while the majority of Republicans wanted to enforce it. But there was a small Republican insurgency that sided with the Democrats – which is why the Republican elephant looks tempted to jump into the trough with the Democrat donkey.

Reporter. " You 're working very hard, aren't you? "
Youthful Film-Star. " Yep; I 'm hoping to retire when I 'm twelve."

The 1934 musical *Stand Up And Cheer!* catapulted six-year-old Shirley Temple to stardom –
less than a year later she was awarded the first Juvenile Oscar for her work. As a result 1930s
Hollywood was hit by a flood of child stars. Among them were the likes of Judy Garland, Deanna
Durbin, Freddie Bartholomew and Mickey Rooney, who this *Punch* cartoon appears to caricature.
Rooney had been appearing in films since 1927.

Titled 'Roosevelt to the Rescue', this 1933 cartoon by Bernard Partridge shows President Roosevelt helping a child (the US dollar) negotiate the currency crisis. Roosevelt had swept to victory in the presidential elections that year, with his campaign theme promising 'Happy Days Are Here Again'. Thanks to Roosevelt's 'New Deal', the US economy improved rapidly from 1933 until 1937, when it was hit by a further recession.

American artist Paule Loring responds to the German federal elections in March 1933, which saw the Nazis emerge as the largest party. Hitler passed the Enabling Act weeks later, giving himself the power to pass laws without involving the Reichstag parliament. It effectively made him dictator of Germany. The 1933 election was the last multi-party election held for the whole country before the reunification of Germany in 1990.

"I WONDER IF IT'S WORTH SEEING?"

A gaggle of representatives from the League of Nations implore Uncle Sam to do something about hostilities between China and Japan. In 1931 Japan invaded Manchuria on China's eastern seaboard in a bid to expand its empire. Winsor McCay's cartoon draws attention to the powerlessness of the League, whose principal mission was to maintain world peace, but also to America's isolationism – clearly, neither want to get involved.

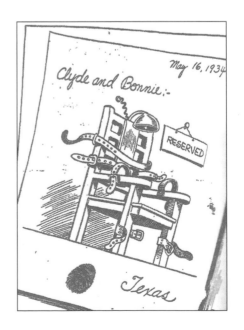

OPPOSITE: Pont responds to his own invented hype with some typical English understatement. This appeared in *Punch* in 1934 during Hollywood's 'Golden Age'.
RIGHT: The *Dallas Journal* ran this cartoon of an electric chair 'reserved' for Bonnie and Clyde in May 1934, several days before the outlaws were ambushed and killed in Louisiana.

INCREASING PRESSURE.

David Low's perceptive cartoon of 18 February 1938 criticizes the decision by the inter-war British and French governments to follow a policy of appeasement with Germany. Low anticipates the domino-effect set in motion by the *Anschluss* (annexation) of Austria into the German Third Reich, which occurred on 12 March 1938. A year later, Germany had occupied all of Czechoslovakia; by September 1939, Britain and Germany were at war.

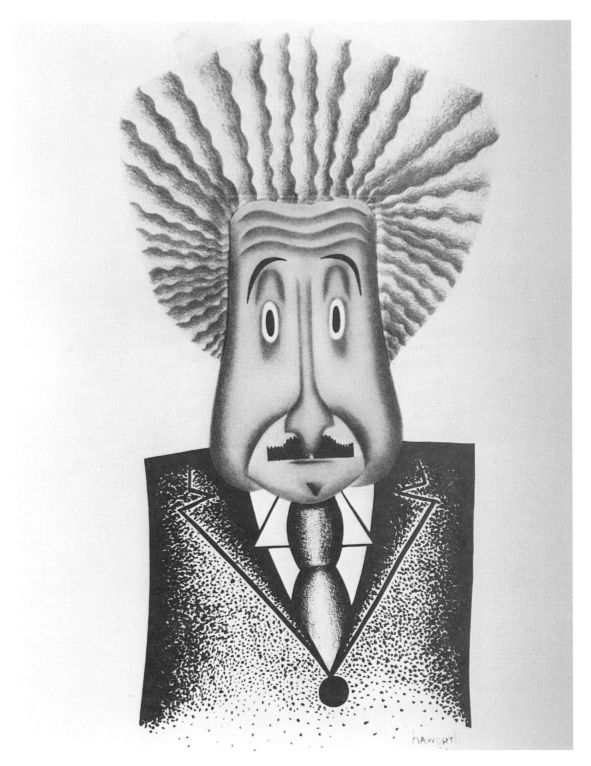

Albert Einstein was one of many German Jewish intellectuals who, barred from entering professions and threatened with their lives, fled to the United States following the rise of the Nazi party. In 1939 Einstein was alerted to the Nazis' research into developing atomic weapons and supported a letter to President Roosevelt, advising that the US begin similar investigations. These eventually led to the Manhattan Project.

THE CHOICE

THE PRIME MINISTER. "ALL THE PEOPLES OF YOUR EMPIRE, SIR, SYMPATHISE WITH YOU MOST DEEPLY ; BUT THEY ALL KNOW—AS YOU YOURSELF MUST—THAT THE THRONE IS GREATER THAN THE MAN."

In 1936 the British monarch, Edward VIII, announced that he was going to marry Wallis Simpson, an American socialite and two-time-divorcee. The match was opposed by the British and Commonwealth governments and threatened to become a constitutional crisis. Bernard Partridge's cartoon for *Punch* shows Prime Minister Stanley Baldwin begging Edward to choose the throne instead of Wallis Simpson.

Winged Victory

COMMEMORATING
THE TRIUMPH OF
ARMY BOMBERS
OVER
NONCOMBATANTS
IN SPAIN AND CHINA

American cartoonist Herb Block ('Herblock') refers to the Greek statue 'Winged Victory of Samothrace' in this image from 1938. Rather than honouring a battle, the cartoon denounces the aerial atrocities committed in Spain and China that year. On the eve of World War II, it was clear that aviation had changed the nature of war. Armies now had the potential to eliminate thousands of civilians from above in the name of combat.

— — **AND THE SEVEN DWARFS**

In 1937 Walt Disney's *Snow White and the Seven Dwarfs* premiered to massive critical acclaim and popular success. In this cartoon for *Punch* published in 1938, Bernard Partridge casts Hitler as Snow White, holding aloft a Nazi swastika, while the countries of Eastern Europe become the Seven Dwarfs, who look on and wonder what the symbol will mean for them.

Adolf Hitler and Soviet dictator Joseph Stalin are presented as greedy cats, eyeing up their next meal (the Balkan countries) in this cartoon from 1939. Romania and Bulgaria joined with Germany and Russia in 1940 and 1941 respectively and Axis forces invaded Yugoslavia and Greece in April 1941.

The 1936 Summer Olympics were held in Berlin, where Hitler famously refused to shake hands with black runner Jesse Owens following his victory in the 100m Sprint because it challenged the notion of Aryan supremacy. This German cartoon shies away from controversy and instead offers a light-hearted take on how the Olympics might look in the year 2000. High-tech TVs will allow spectators to watch the events at home and have their applause conveyed through loudspeakers into the stadium.

'Take me to Czechoslovakia, Driver': in March 1938, following the annexation of Austria, Hitler was turning his attention towards the Sudeten area of Czechoslovakia. Printed in the *Chicago Times* in 1938 this cartoon by Vaughn Shoemaker was dubbed by Hermann Goering a 'horrible example of anti-Nazi propaganda'.

1940s

The 1940s were a turbulent decade and they marked a turning point in history. Once fascism was defeated, the Western nations were able to lay the foundations for a new kind of democracy. For some nations, it was a case of one step forward, two steps back. The Soviet Union built an 'iron curtain' dividing Europe in two. In 1947, India was partitioned and Israel was founded. A year later, Gandhi was assassinated, McCarthy began his 'witch hunts' in the US and apartheid was imposed in South Africa. In 1949, the Soviet Union detonated its first nuclear bomb and Mao Zedong won the civil war in China as Chiang Kai-shek went off and founded a separate state in Taiwan. All this provided perfect material for cartoonists.

'His Servant's Voice' (1945) by Leslie Illingworth: at this point in the war, there was a suggestion that Hitler was no longer in control of Germany and that Himmler had taken over the reins.

Pont (Graham Laidler) was one of the great chroniclers of the British way of life. He trained at the London School of Architecture, but was never able to practise the profession because of illness. He still put his draughtsmanship to good use in the service of *Punch* magazine, gently mocking the foibles of his fellow human beings. He died in 1940 of poliomyelitis. This was his take on Europe from listening to his radio that same year.

Churchill called Jane 'Britain's secret weapon'. Drawn by Norman Pett and modelled by Chrystabel Leighton-Porter, she was a true Forces Sweetheart with her Dachshund Fritz. Despite being a cartoon character she received endless proposals of marriage from servicemen. The formula was simple: when times were bad, she shed more clothes. When she first appeared naked in 1944, it was said she inspired the British army to advance six miles into Burma.

ABOVE AND BELOW: Cartoons from *Das Reich* magazine, a weekly magazine started by Josef Goebbels in 1940 whose circulation peaked at 1.4 million. The top one (1940) shows a typical British aristocrat attempting to reject socialism and being told he will just have to swallow it – note the handy spittoon. The other (1944) shows the V-1 rocket or Buzz Bomb. The Germans weren't finished with such a weapon up their sleeve…

RIGHT: 'Churchill's New Year's Day Hangover' (1942 – *Katzenjammer* means 'the wailing of cats' and 'hangover' in German): rancid alleycats crawl all over Churchill in this drawing by Erich Schilling as he tries to recover from consuming too much home-made punch made from lies and illusions. Passing reference is also made on the cats' collars to the recent loss of HMS *Repulse* and *Prince of Wales*. Schilling, who loved drawing Churchill as a drunk, committed suicide in 1945 when the war was lost.

Churchills Silvesterkatzenjammer

(Erich Schilling)

„Goddam, wie ist mir mein Lügen- und Illusionspunsch schlecht bekommen!!"

Churchill dopo la sbornia di San Silvestro: "Goddam! . . . Come m'ha fatto male il ponce delle menzogne e delle illusioni!,,

4

IMPROVING THE RACE
Selected breed of delegates for Nazi Congress
Cartoon by Yefimov, 1941

FIB-DETECTORS
German Command's Report of Military Operations
Cartoon by Kukryniksy, 1941

ARABIAN TALES
Cartoon by Kukryniksy, 1941

THE NAZI KENNEL
Cartoon by Kukryniksy, 1941

Russian cartoonists did not hold back when it came to rubbishing the Nazis during World War II. Top left on this page is a drawing by Boris Yefimov ridiculing the idea of the master race as represented by those in the Nazi party. The other three cartoons are by Kukryniksy, the name adopted by three caricaturists, Mikhail Kuprilianov, Porfirii Krylov and Nikolai Solokov, who met at art school in the 1920s and established their own collective.

'Leaders of the Master Race' (c.1941) by Boris Yefimov: Yefimov was Stalin's favourite cartoonist and the great tyrant sent him ideas for cartoons, often with minuscule deadlines attached. Later, Yefimov produced Cold War propaganda and died in 2008 aged 108.

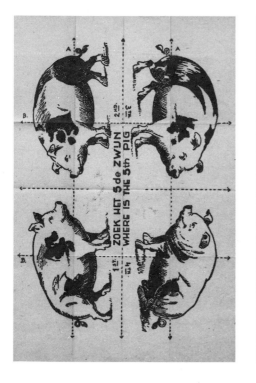

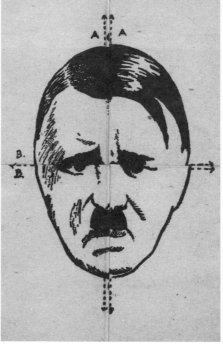

A subversive little puzzle from occupied Holland: the question – 'Where is the 5th pig?' – could be answered by making the correct folds in the original picture (far left), to create a new image (near left). Neat, but not the kind of thing you wanted to be caught with.

... and the Wolf chewed up the children and spit out their bones ...
But those were <u>Foreign Children</u> and it really didn't matter."

'Adolf the Wolf' (1941) by Dr Seuss: the US organization against American entry into World War II, America First, is represented by a mother reading a fairytale aloud to her children, who along with the family cat appear a trifle alarmed at what they are hearing. During wartime, Dr Seuss (Theodor Geisel) turned out over 400 cartoons for New York daily, *PM*, many of them urging the US government to send its forces against the Nazis.

Mussolini

Herb Block produced these vignettes of Mussolini's life, illustrating constant aggression, after he blamed defeat in Libya on the fact that the British attacked before the Italian army was ready. Block's cartoons provide a running commentary on US history. He became a much-loved national watchdog, keeping a wary eye on what politicians were up to and drawing his opinions with a freedom that might not have been tolerated in words.

FROM THE BALTIC TO THE BLACK

D. R. Fitzpatrick always drew with a grease crayon. His cartoons were never funny, rather he was a master of symbolism. He started warning the US about the dangers of fascism in the 1930s and, by characterizing the Third Reich as a giant death machine, played a part in persuading his country to rethink its isolationist stance a decade later. In this image (1941) the swastika stalls on the Eastern Front against the combined might of millions.

In this cartoon from 1942, Fitzpatrick shows, with a certain grim satisfaction, the German army marching relentlessly towards their own deaths in Stalingrad. The Battle of Stalingrad marked a turning point in World War II; for the first time the German army had been defeated on the field of battle. Before Stalingrad, the Russians had never won; after Stalingrad they could not lose.

A travelogue of life in the New Zealand Expeditionary Forces in Egypt and Italy during World War II by Neville Colvin who was a cartoonist with the *Wellington Evening Post*. It makes the whole business of war seem rather like a jolly tourist trip to Europe, even if there are occasional hints of dark encounters with the enemy. Colvin moved to London after the war and drew the *Modesty Blaise* strip from 1980 to 1986.

"... Meanwhile, in Britain, the entire population faced by the threat of invasion, has been flung into a state of complete panic ... etc., etc., etc."

ABOVE: Pont was a master of understatement and perhaps his most famous cartoon was of the English pub in 1940, where life carries on regardless despite the imminent possibility of invasion by the Nazis.

ABOVE LEFT: Johnny Canuck was a lumberjack when he first turned up as the living embodiment of Canada in 1869. He was reinvented as an action hero by cartoonist Leo Bachle for Bell's *Dime Comics* in February 1941 and went on to win the war virtually single-handed after a brief encounter with Adolf Hitler.

LEFT: 'An Australian Serviceman Catches His Wife with a US Serviceman' (1943) by P. F. C. Davisson: the title may be prosaic but it tells all. GIs started arriving in Australia in 1941 and brought with them alcohol, chewing gum, cigarettes and nylon stockings, giving them immense pulling power. More than 12,000 Australian women ended up marrying US soldiers.

"...SHALL NOT HAVE DIED IN VAIN"

In a solemn moment at the end of the war in 1945, D. R. Fitzpatrick evokes the spirit of the Gettysburg Address of 1863 by Abraham Lincoln. America's entry into the newly established United Nations organization was seen as the peaceful way ahead for the world, and something that would make the sacrifice of so many brave servicemen worthwhile. This was a time for reflection rather than triumphalism.

'A New Era in Man's Understanding of Nature's Forces' (1945) by D. R. Fitzpatrick: after the bombing of Hiroshima, President Truman took the decision to drop a further atomic bomb on Nagasaki in August 1945. The Atomic Age had arrived and, from this point on, the USSR rushed to develop its own nuclear bomb, so it could maintain parity with the US, a disconcerting turn of events after the triumphant ending of the war. You weren't safe after all.

'A peep under the Iron Curtain' (1946) by Leslie Illingworth, first published in the *Daily Mail*. Many historians consider that Winston Churchill's 'iron curtain' speech in March 1946 marked the start of the Cold War. It certainly inspired this cartoon, which shows Churchill defying Josef Stalin's order by trying to steal a glimpse into the forbidden land that flies the hammer and sickle flag and lies beyond the barrier suddenly dividing Europe in two. Normal traffic has ceased – as indicated by the railway line to nowhere – and Eastern Europe is a vast prison complete with guards along its perimeter.

THE INDIAN "WORKING PARTY"

The British Cabinet sent a delegation to India in 1946 to discuss the division of the country into 'Hindu-majority India and Muslim-majority India'. Illingworth imagined those concerned on the back of this elephant: Nehru, Mahatma Gandhi, Stafford Cripps, Pethick-Lawrence et al, debating away. Partition occurred in 1947 as hundreds of thousands were displaced and the Dominion of Pakistan and the Union of India came into being.

" Happy new ration book, madam ! "

Cartoonist Frank Reynolds was brilliant at drawing characters and this offering from 1945 perfectly evokes the era just after the end of the war. Even the dog has personality. In 1948 bread rationing ended; 1950 marked the end of petrol rationing; and in 1954 meat and all other food rationing ceased. Ration books were a much-valued currency and there were many cases where the living fraudulently held on to the ration books of the dead.

In 1947, the House Committee of Un-American Activities held nine days of hearings into alleged communist propaganda in Hollywood, but the dress rehearsal for the infamous witch hunt took place six years earlier. The cartoon above by Jim Berryman (son of Clifford) was published in the *Washington Evening Star* in 1941 after senators Burton Wheeler and Gerald Nye of the isolationist America First movement went to work on Charlie Chaplin's anti-fascist film, *The Great Dictator* (1941), calling it '[part of a] violent propaganda campaign intending to incite the American people to the point where they will become involved in this war [WWII]'. In the event, Chaplin was never called upon to testify before the committee because Pearl Harbor intervened, but later in the decade, when 300 artists were blacklisted as communists, he left for Switzerland, never to return.

After the USSR tested its first atomic bomb known as 'First Lightning' in 1949 – pretty much an exact copy of the US Fat Man design, incorporating leaked information from Los Alamos – the idea that there were Soviet spies everywhere gathered pace. Everyone was a suspect: even teachers in elementary schools, even Thomas Jefferson, the great advocate of freedom of speech! Here Herb Block tells us how over the top the reaction was.

العراق العربي الاصيل ..

« الانكليز بعد أن يرميهم العراق أرضاً يهزأ فيهم العالم و يخاطبهم بقوله :
— ولكم انتم مجانين ؟! ليش هذا حصان ركوب لو حصان ... ؟..

Britain first left Iraq, which it had set up, in 1932, but resumed control in 1941 when pro-Axis generals returned Rashid Ali to power. This cartoon, with John Bull being thrown by a fiery Arab stallion marked 'Iraq', dates from that time. The British left Iraq again in 1947.

OLD LOW'S ALMANACK — PROPHECIES for 1949

J.B.S. Haldane, refusing to recant utterly, is denounced by the DAILY WORKER as a bourgeois pseudo-scientist.

J. B. S. Haldane was an English genetic scientist and Marxist, who served as chairman on the *Daily Worker* editorial board. Haldane became disillusioned at the persecution of geneticists in the Soviet Union under Lysenko and Stalin. Here, David Low foresees his show trial: Haldane's braces are taken off to rob him of human dignity like Stalin's victims, and there is even a joke about Lamarckian plant breeding favoured by communists.

HOW TO CLOSE THE GAP?

'How to close the gap?' (1948) by D. R. Fitzpatrick: this is a comment on the bear grip Russia held over Berlin after WWII – there was only one road in. When the Soviets sought complete control over the former German capital by blocking rail, road and canal access, the Berlin Blockade began. It lasted from June 1948 until May 1949 and Allied airforces flew over 200,000 missions, delivering vital supplies into the beleaguered western sector and eventually forcing the Russians to relax their grip. It was hailed as a victory for the 'free world'.

'I knew we should have kept on Route 66 out of Flagstaff' (1947) by Sam Cobean: Cobean worked as an inbetweener on Walt Disney's *Snow White*, was best friends with Charles Addams and is generally credited with inventing the cartoonist's thought bubble when he worked for *The New Yorker*. Cobean loved travelling round America with his wife in their red Jaguar and it may have inspired this surprise excursion into a Dali landscape.

WITH APOLOGIES TO WALT DISNEY

Legendary cartoonist Edwin Marcus depicts the standoff between Joseph Stalin and
Yugoslavian leader Josip Broz Tito, which would last until the mid-1950s. Stalin wanted
Yugoslavia to become a Soviet satellite state, but Tito was having none of it.

1950s

The 1950s saw the start of a very different type of conflict in the form of the Cold War. The rivalry between the Soviet Union and America even extended beyond the Earth's atmosphere, with satellites and monkeys being launched into space. The Korean War (1950–53) dragged on and Joseph Stalin died (1953). Most American households acquired a TV – 80 million watched the anti-communist McCarthy hearings in 1954 – but film studios drew audiences back to the cinema with the help of stars like John Wayne and James Stewart and technology such as VistaVision. As scientists carried out nuclear tests in the Pacific, rock'n'roll exploded across the US. Inventions included credit cards, Barbie dolls and 'the teenager'.

"You Mean I'm Supposed To Stand On That?"

This cartoon by Herb Block coined the term 'McCarthyism' and appeared in the *Washington Post* on 29 March 1950, shortly after Senator Joseph McCarthy began his infamous anti-communist witch hunts. Herb Block drew from a liberal perspective and his work throughout the 1950s targets McCarthy and his supporters. Here, the Republican elephant is forced towards an election platform, balanced on top of McCarthy's smear campaign.

Leo Joseph Roche encapsulates the public uproar that greeted President Harry S. Truman's decision to sack General Douglas MacArthur, popular commander of US forces in Korea, in April 1951. Among several dangerous proposals, MacArthur wanted to bomb China, but Truman was determined to fight a 'limited war' in Korea, a position which is now seen as very sensible. ('John Q' is the US version of 'Joe Public'.)

THE ACTORS' SYMPOSIUM
(a) THE GREEN ROOM BAR

THE ACTORS' SYMPOSIUM
(b) THE CELLULOID CAFETERIA

The British acting fraternity was wont to frown upon its Hollywood brethren, even though many were forced to 'slum it' before the cameras in search of fame and fortune. The contrasting worlds of 'proper actors' (British, of course, darling) and their US screen counterparts is captured in these cartoons by Ronald Searle and Robert Sherriffs. Opposite you can see the likes of John Gielgud, Margaret Rutherford and Laurence Olivier, whereas above you'll find old friends like Orson Welles, Marlene Dietrich and even Mickey Mouse.

'Empty Shoes' by David Low appeared in the *Manchester Guardian* on 6 March 1953, the day after Joseph Stalin died. Stalin had reportedly fallen ill following an all-night dinner on 1 March. He didn't emerge from his room the next day but his aides were too afraid to disturb him, so medical assistance was delayed. Here Stalin's potential successors, Lavrentiy Beria and Georgy Malenkov, tentatively move to fill his shoes.

Red to play and mate in one

Leslie Illingworth translates the political and military situation in Vietnam on to the chess board in this cartoon from 1954. That year the country was partitioned into North and South following the Geneva Agreements. The cartoon registers Russia's manoeuvres to take Vietnam, presented here as the quickest checkmate in chess.

"Of course I know what I'm doing."

Victor Weisz (aka 'Vicky') was a German-British cartoonist who came to the UK in 1935 following the rise to power of the Nazi party, and contributed work to the *Daily Mirror, Telegraph* and the *Evening Standard*. In this cartoon from 1954, Vicky reacts to the US tests of a hydrogen bomb at Bikini Atoll in the Pacific. The explosion was believed to have been 1,000 times more powerful than the atomic bomb that destroyed Hiroshima in 1945.

"... *that we here highly resolve ... that this nation, under God, shall have a new birth of freedom.*"
Abraham Lincoln at Gettysburg

Leslie Illingworth notes Senator McCarthy's rapid fall in popularity in this cartoon from 1954, by which point the Senator had begun to lose the support of US public opinion. That year the Army-McCarthy hearings received widespread TV coverage, and McCarthy was presented in a particularly unfavourable light.

Leslie Illingworth's response to the Egyptian Suez Crisis of 1956. President Nasser is compared to the Biblical figure of Salome, receiving the head of UK Prime Minister Anthony Eden who resigned from office in January 1957 over his handling of the crisis. Britain, France and Israel had launched a joint attack on Egypt in an attempt to regain Western control of the Suez Canal, but they had been forced into a humiliating withdrawal following pressure from America, the USSR and the United Nations.

OPPOSITE: The collective leadership that replaced Stalin in 1953 introduced a process of 'de-Stalinization' in the Soviet Union, dismantling the institutions that had kept him in power, such as the Gulag labour camps. Here Leslie Illingworth references the destruction of Stalin's statue by anti-Soviet protesters during Hungary's October Revolution of 1956.

In the 1950s more than 50 per cent of fatalities on American roads involved drunk drivers. Police departments were desperate to combat the problem, but determining whether someone was too drunk to drive was highly subjective. The invention of the first 'Breathalyzer' by Robert Frank Borkenstein in 1954 was a breakthrough, providing police with a simple, scientific means of tackling drunk driving.

IKE'S DRUM
Ike is in his bunker and three thousand miles away
(Capten, art tha sleepin' there below?)

Leslie Illingworth alludes to a poem about 16th century explorer Francis Drake and his legendary drum, which will beat at times of national crisis. Drake famously finished playing a game of bowls on Plymouth Hoe before defeating the Spanish Armada. In this 1956 cartoon golf-fanatic President Dwight 'Ike' Eisenhower takes in a round before dealing with pressing affairs of state (i.e. the Cold War).

American cartoonist Russell Brockbank shows a group of nervous monkeys drawing lots to decide who will be the first to fly into space. On 13 December 1958 NASA launched a rocket from Cape Canaveral with a South American squirrel monkey named Gordo on board. The craft exited and re-entered the Earth's atmosphere but Gordo's parachute failed and his body was never recovered. The following year Miss Able and Miss Baker became the first monkeys to survive a spaceflight – Miss Baker lived until 1984.

New Zealand cartoonist Neville Colvin responds to a criticism of Wellington women's fashion sense in this sketch from 1954. Christian Dior's H-line – a slender tunic suit with a slim skirt – became one of the most iconic styles of the decade. Here, Colvin likens its explosive impact on fashion to the H-bomb.

Born Marion Morrison in 1907, actor John Wayne became one of the most famous American film stars of the 20th century. This *Punch* cartoon shows Wayne in his role as tenacious Civil War veteran Ethan Edwards in John Ford's *The Searchers* (1956). The film was a massive commercial success and is consistently ranked as the greatest Western of all time. The cowboys-and-indians-craze flourished in school playgrounds throughout the 1950s.

'Confuse us, he say…' by Emmwood (1958): Chinese leader Mao Zedong assumes the pose of Buddha and the cartoonist nods to Confucius, while Nikita Khrushchev, Charles de Gaulle, Harold Macmillan and Dwight Eisenhower puzzle over how to deal with China. In 1958 Mao launched his 'Great Leap Forward', a ruthless economic campaign resulting in the Great Chinese Famine and the deaths of some 45 million people.

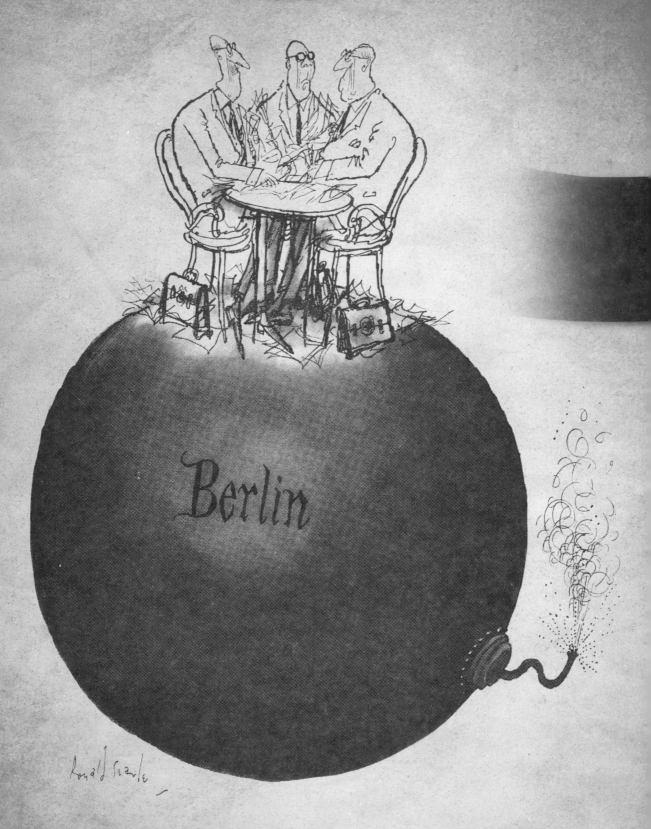

A few days after the East German authorities began building the Berlin Wall, diplomats from Britain, Russia and the US met in Geneva to talk about nuclear disarmament. It wasn't a good time for discussions and the USSR resumed nuclear testing immediately afterwards

1960s

The Swinging Sixties saw social upheaval in the West as young people questioned the values of previous generations. In Africa, 32 countries gained independence from their colonial rulers, the Bay of Pigs fiasco embarrassed the US and the Cuban Missile Crisis almost led to the destruction of the world. Kennedy, Martin Luther King, Jr. and Malcolm X were assassinated, Che Guevara was executed and nightly news footage of the Vietnam War delivered the horrific reality to every TV set in the US. Mankind also landed on the Moon. The 'counterculture' affected attitudes of all kinds and led men to have long hair, women to wear mini skirts and people to lead their lives in what they believed was a whole new 'liberated' way.

HERE WE GO AGAIN

Ed Valtman '60

A Democrat donkey and a Republican elephant as drawn by Ed Valtman in 1960 – they're competing organ-grinders in the TV age, each one with a monkey begging for votes. The first TV presidential election debate took place in 1960. Nixon failed to wear make-up and came across as seedy and unshaven (just like he did in Herb Block's cartoons). John F. Kennedy was the telegenic glamour boy who narrowly edged victory.

RIGHT: Assegais sprout from the ground in the wake of the apartheid tractor. Reap as ye sow is the Biblical message of this brilliant cartoon by Norman Mansbridge. It was published just before the Sharpeville Massacre in 1960, when 69 black South Africans were shot dead by police.

DRAGON'S TEETH

"You're New Here, Aren't You?"

HERBLOCK
©1961 THE WASHINGTON POST CO.

The GDR started building the Berlin Wall on 13 August 1961. The idea was to cut West Berlin off from its surroundings to prevent East Germans from escaping. In the East, they called it 'the Anti-Fascist Protection Rampart'; in the West, it was 'the Wall of Shame'. In any other terms, it was the Iron Curtain rendered in concrete. Herb Block clarifies the issue by having a single East German policeman face the wrong way.

PUNCH, July 19 1961

LEFT: Ban the Bomb marches were a common sight in Britain in the 1960s. They briefly became part of the nation's Easter calendar from 1958 to 1965 as diehards marched the 53 miles from the Aldermaston Atomic Weapons plant in Hampshire to central London. Crowds reached 150,000 at the rallying point in Trafalgar Square.

BELOW: In 1962, following the Bay of Pigs, Cuba asked for, and got, Russian protection in the form of nuclear missiles. A tense standoff ensued between the US and the USSR as the rest of the world watched on in horror, captured here by Illingworth as a bout of arm-wrestling between JFK and Khrushchev with each man's finger hovering above the nuclear button. Eventually the Russians relented and removed their weaponry from Cuba.

Two very different views of Cuba: the top one, by Ed Valtman (1961), shows a boastful Fidel Castro with two figures: Cuba (in chains) and Brazil, whom he is trying to seduce. Below is 'Hoarders' by an unknown Cuban postcard artist of the 1960s. This is an amusing memento of the time just after the Revolution. Here, a cockahoop Fidel Castro is portrayed as the (macho) man who gets the girls in his small proletarian open-top which is overtaking the capitalist – or hoarder – in his massive American automobile. The message? That the revolutionaries are carrying all before them and the US gangsters who ran Havana with its casino culture under Batista will no longer have things their way. Interestingly, many fabulous American cars from the 1950s and 1960s are still being driven around Cuba, much polished, lovingly repaired and now running on a wing and a prayer.

BETTER RELATIONS THROUGH TRADE

ABEL   POWERS

Ed Valtman '62
The Hartford Times

Gary Powers was the American pilot of a Lockheed U-2 spy plane shot down over Soviet territory in 1960 and sentenced to 10 years; Rudolf Abel was a Soviet intelligence officer found guilty of spying in the US. Ed Valtman shows the exchange of prisoners that took place in 1962 on Glienicke Bridge, Berlin, a setting which was used for trades between the two sides, including humans rights activist Anatoly Sharansky in 1968. The title is ironic.

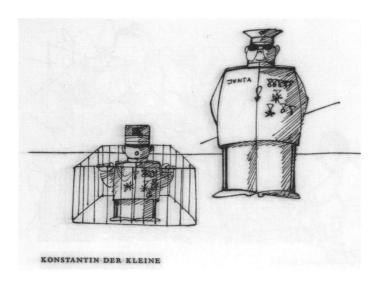

KONSTANTIN DER KLEINE

'Little Constantine' (1967): a German cartoon shows Greek king Constantine II under the control of the generals. Eventually the king organized a counter-coup against the military junta who had taken over the country, but he had to flee Greece and go into exile, losing his crown for ever.

"Next time, Comrade Gagarin, where these red-coloured glasses!"

In 1961 Yuri Gagarin became the first man in space, chalking up a huge propaganda victory for the USSR and demanding put-downs in response from the West at the height of the Cold War. This cartoon appeared in Australian newspaper *The Herald* and was drawn by John Frith.

"PERHAPS IF WE JUST SHUT THE DOOR IT WILL GO AWAY."

The first oral contraceptive pill became available in the early 1960s, creating a problem for the Catholic Church, who refused to move on the issue of birth control and suddenly seemed out of step with the times as this drawing by John Jensen shows. Remarkably, the debate still goes on today.

BIG MAN ON THE CAMPUS

In 1961, following the admission of two black students, Charlayne Hunter and Hamilton Holmes, there were riots at the University of Georgia. Clifford Baldowski drew a Frankenstein monster carrying a rock in each hand and wearing a college sweatshirt labelled 'Mob Violence'. Civil rights were a big issue in the 1960s, as was desegregation of education. In 1962, the Supreme Court ruled segregation in public schools unconstitutional.

"I Still Can't Believe It"

©1963 HERBLOCK
THE WASHINGTON POST

The cliché was to ask, 'Where were you when you heard about the death of President Kennedy?' The answer, for many Americans, was that they were home watching TV and in this drawing Herb Block captured the horror they felt. It was the day when America seemed to lose its innocence and faith in the future. The doomladen mood intensified when JFK's alleged assassin, Lee Harvey Oswald, received a mortal bullet wound live on TV.

De Gaulle once described the Jewish people as 'domineering and sure of itself', which prompted MIT (Louis Mitelberg, Poland-born, Jewish-French cartoonist and caricaturist) to come up with this portrait of the French president, based loosely on a painting by Rembrandt of 'Aristotle with a bust of blind, humble Homer'. There's nothing humble about the figure of de Gaulle here.

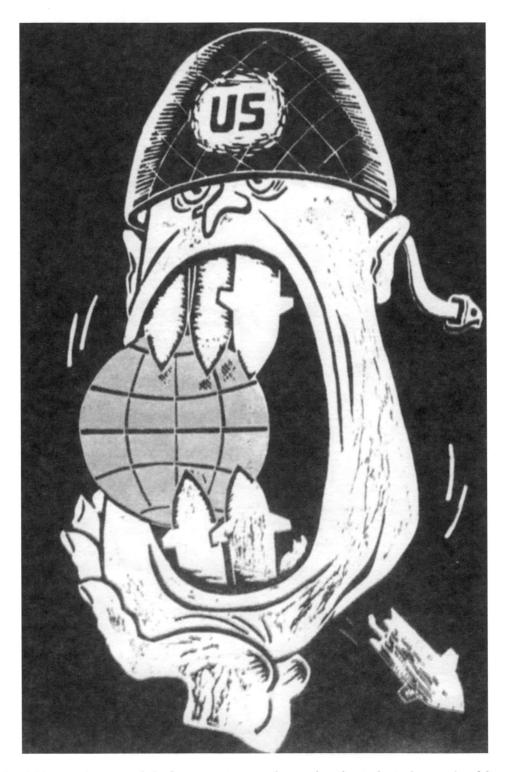

During the Cold War, it became a cliché for cartoonists to replace teeth with missiles in the mouths of the military. This Russian image shows an American soldier trying to chew up the world with his new gnashers. At the start of the 1960s people talked about the policy of MAD (mutually assured destruction): the US had over 30,000 nuclear missiles, the USSR 5,000. A mushroom cloud seemed to be hovering not far away.

After the British helped to set up the Federation of Malaysia in 1963, President Sukarno of Indonesia boasted he would crush the fledgling state by the time the cock crowed at dawn on 1 January 1965 and sent in his troops. This cartoon was released to newspapers for publication by the Malaysian government on 31 December 1964. In 1967 Sukarno was put under house arrest by his own army and he died of kidney failure in 1970.

A cartoon from 1969 by Ed McLachlan about the dangers of taking LSD. McLachlan himself seemed to be drawing under the influence of the Beatles' *Yellow Submarine* cartoon (1968).

"We have reason to believe you are carrying certain substances of a hallucinogenic nature."

In 1969, avant-garde artist Yoko Ono married John Lennon and they spent their honeymoon in Amsterdam holding a 'bed-in' for peace. Not long after that they recorded 'Give Peace a Chance' in Montreal. The couple became the subject of worldwide gossip. After *Abbey Road*, the Beatles were beginning to disintegrate and Ono was blamed by many for the break-up. To this day, some people have never forgiven her.

Michael Atchison's drawing (from January, 1967) of Muhammad Ali in anticipation of his joining the US Army. In the event, Ali refused to be inducted – 'I ain't got no quarrel with them Vietcong' – and was rapidly stripped of his heavyweight title. Atchison never used pencil lines, always drawing ink straight on to paper.

In 1965, the first US combat troops began to arrive in Vietnam to supplement the US advisors already in place. It was soon obvious that America would have a hard time extricating itself from the situation which is graphically portrayed by Vaughn Shoemaker as President Lyndon Johnson clings on for dear life to the tail of a tiger. The US didn't pull out of Vietnam until 1973, by which time 60,000 Americans and 2 million Vietnamese had died.

Uncle Sam tries to keep his head above water and his M-16 rifle dry as he wades through the swamp of war in Asia. Herb Block neatly summed up the doubt in the minds of the US public which was ceasing to believe the Johnson adminstration knew what it was doing in Indochina. In 1968, the North Vietnamese army had launched the Tet offensive with the aim of bringing down the Saigon government and scuppering US hopes in the region.

ENGLISH VERSION front cover -- Click below for Spanish, or http://www.ep.tc/mlk
1956 Martin Luther King Jr "Montgomery Story" comic book - Civil rights pamphlet
used for proselytizing the story of MLK and Rosa Parks, as well as the ideas of
Passive Resistance to other civil rights workers in the 1950s - http://www.ep.tc

The cover of a comic book biography of Martin Luther King, hero of the civil rights movement in the US: King practised civil disobedience and non-violent protest based on Christian beliefs. He was famous for his 'I have a dream' speech, but was assassinated by James Earl Ray in Memphis, Tennessee, after which riots broke out in many US cities.

General Yakkubu Gowon drives a wooden stake into the heart of Biafra, the eastern region of Nigeria which had attempted to declare independence. The civil war that ensued lasted 30 months and caused the death of 100,000 soldiers and over a million civilians, most of whom died of starvation because of the blockade imposed by the government. This drawing by Ed McLachlan appeared in *Punch* in 1969.

THE NEW IMPERIALISTS

To commemorate the first man on the Moon in 1969, Ralph Steadman gently reminded us that the space race had become a new kind of imperialism.

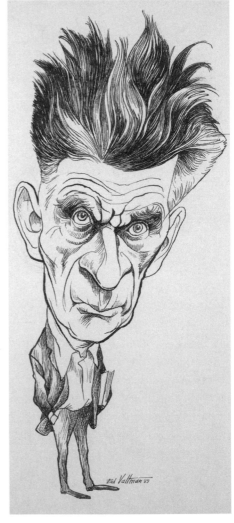

Ed Valtman's cartoon of Samuel Beckett, book under arm and eagle-like gaze to the fore. Beckett won the 1969 Nobel Prize in Literature for 'his writing which – in new forms of the novel and drama – acquires its elevation in the destitution of mankind'. Beckett was most famous for his play *Waiting for Godot*, a sublime exercise in tragi-comedy and gallows humour.

When Georges Pompidou succeeded De Gaulle as French president in 1969, his predecessor's veto was lifted and Britain was able to start applying for the Common Market. This is recorded rather nicely by Ed Mclachlan as British Prime Minister Harold Wilson climbs through an enormous 'NON' waving his British flag. The British, being an island race, have always had an uneasy relationship with Europe and this remains true today.

BRITNIK 1

Ed McLachlan's design for the first British space station (1969) is an exuberant display of British nonsense. The 1960s had been a great decade for Britain and now it was all coming to an end: the Beatles had given their last performance, England had won the soccer World Cup in 1966, and Britain had won the Eurovision Song Contest twice… would things ever be as good again?

With the imminence of the Apollo XII launch, Britain has finally decided to get in on the space act. The first British space station, entirely designed by McLACHLAN, is due to go into orbit any decade now.

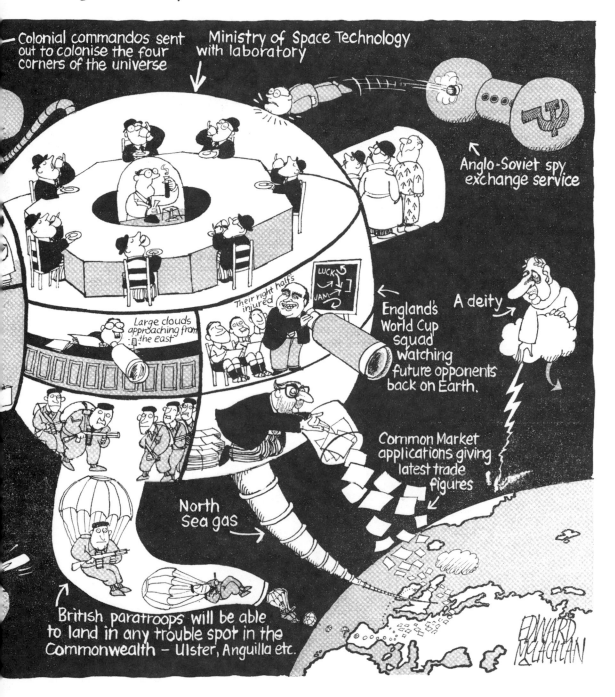

Richard Nixon entangled in his web of lies in a cartoon by Robert Pryor (1974). Nixon was the first US president ever to be impeached. His transcripts of conversations about Watergate, and extensive use of the term 'expletive deleted', proved a gift for satirists.

1970s

The 'Me Decade' was marked by the first face-lifts, the arrival of the Sony Walkman and the introduction of in vitro fertilization. Politically, it was business as usual, with major energy crises in the West, the Iranian Revolution, the Soweto uprising, mass murder in Pol Pot's Cambodia and Idi Amin's Uganda, and General Pinochet extinguishing democracy in Chile. Margaret Thatcher was elected the first female Prime Minister of the UK, Mao Zedong died, the Soviet Union invaded Afghanistan and Japan became, briefly, the world's leading industrial power. On the fashion front the 1970s will always be remembered: for over-the-top perms, platform soles and ludicrously long shirt collars which flapped in the wind.

British Prime Minister Ted Heath is a docker who's just packed up a new consignment of arms for the apartheid regime in South Africa, 1971. African regimes at the Commonwealth Conference failed to prevent the UK from continuing such sales and it was a massive bone of contention at home and abroad. The drawing is by Bill Papas and the little mouse puffing on a cigarette by the packing case was his alter ego, appearing often in his work.

"Heathen bloody savages!"

The Northern Ireland 'Troubles' were always in the headlines in the 1970s, with bombings, shootings and atrocities of all kinds committed more or less on a daily basis. Here Trog, aka Wally Fawkes, is making the point that, shocking as events were in Uganda, the violence from the IRA was just as bad. Fawkes, creator of Flook, was a wayward, unpredictable talent. He worked mainly for the *Daily Mail* and was Mrs Thatcher's favourite cartoonist.

"Look—Nice Tapes—Okay, Boy?—Okay?—"

©1973 HERBLOCK

Herb Block said, 'If the prime role of a free press is to serve as critic of the government, cartooning is often the cutting edge of that criticism.' When ex-workers of Nixon's re-election campaign were arrested for breaking into the Democrat HQ in the Watergate building in 1972, it led to scandal. 'Tricky' Dicky Nixon had been up to all sorts of wrongdoing and release of the tapes recorded in his office only made impeachment more certain.

Israel Prime Minister Golda Meir and Egyptian President Anwar Sadat stand implacably opposed on either side of a giant hour glass. In 1972 Sadat realigned with the West and kicked his Soviet advisers out of the country. Meir took this as a sign that he might be ready for peace talks with Israel, but he turned her down, describing her offer as 'propaganda'. This move was later seen as the first step on the way to the Camp David agreement of 1978.

HOSTAGE

U.S.A.

U.S. GOVT. FAILURE TO END DEPENDENCE ON FOREIGN OIL

© 1979 HERBLOCK

Famous image from the second oil crisis of the decade in 1979, which followed the drop in output after the Iran Revolution. A year later, the Iran-Iraq war caused more uncertainty, but Mexico, Nigeria and Venezuela rode to the rescue of the US, to quench its huge gas-guzzling thirst, when they came on stream with more oil. Because of this, the power of OPEC diminished and Americans began to buy small, fuel-efficient Japanese cars.

'New Internal Combustion Engine' (1973): an ironic Russian response to the oil crisis by Kukryniksy was to invent this quaint, bio-mechanical hybrid vehicle, which you feed at one end and clean up after at the other.

In 1974, times were tough in the UK: the world economy was in turmoil, oil prices had quintupled, and Britain was on a three-day week and facing hyperinflation. Enter Dennis Healey, Chancellor of the Exchequor, little red briefcase in hand. Cartoonist John Jensen, borrowing generously from a popular film poster of 1973, expresses a lack of confidence in the impending budget to be delivered by the man with the caterpillar eyebrows.

'OK, I'M READY AND WILLING TO CARRY THIS OUT'

In 1965, old-fashioned colonialist Ian Smith had unilaterally declared independence for Southern Rhodesia from Great Britain. In 1976 after international sanctions had nearly squeezed the life out of his economy, Smith reluctantly agreed to Henry Kissinger and James Callaghan's plan to transfer power to the black majority within two years. Zimbabwe finally gained independence under Robert Mugabe and a new saga of repression began…

ESTONIAN FOOD PRODUCTION

THE MAN WHO CAME TO DINNER

Valtman'79

Ed Valtman was Estonian and he never forgot his country of origin. After Estonia was coerced into joining the Soviet Union, mass deportations took place and hundreds of thousands of Russians came in to replace the exiles. By 1979, the population was about a quarter Russian and there was a popular play doing the rounds about a greedy and unpleasant man who arrived for dinner and could not be persuaded to leave.

"I see we got our moon rock samples without any risk to human life."

Unmanned Russian space probe Luna 16 landed on the Moon in 1970 to collect mineral samples 'without endangering human life', as Soviet propagandists put it. Cartoonist Bill Tidy took the opportunity to remind *Punch* readers of the USSR's record on human rights. Alexander Solzhenitsyn's *One Day in the Life of Ivan Denisovich* appeared in 1962 and the popularity of this work ensured that most people in the West were aware of the systematic cruelty in operation behind the Iron Curtain.

In this cartoon of 1976 Valtman neatly suggests that the gun control bill had been booby-trapped by the gun lobby.

*"Our token Black—is that really how you think of yourself,
Ms Corwin? You're much more than that, I assure you.
You're also our token woman."*

The 1970s saw the dawning of 'political awareness'. This *Punch* cartoon by Bud Handelsman
turned expectations on their head in what you might think was a thoroughly English way.
Not so. Handelsman was born in the Bronx but came to England believing his style was better
suited to the vein of humour across The Pond. He packed a lot into every frame and his
cartoons on death were renowned.

"I'd better warn the passengers, Chief. We seem to have inadvertently violated Hugh Hefner's air space."

Englishman Ray Lowry was a brilliant chronicler of the excesses of rock'n'roll. In 1979 he toured the US with the Clash as their designated 'war artist'. He liked to work with a Gillott nib (which accounted for the thick swells of Indian ink he achieved) and his style was painterly if often littered with dollops of satirical splatter. This image dates from 1976, when the Stones used a private plane the size of a commercial liner to tour the US. Their tours were the stuff of legend. They were treated like royalty everywhere they went, which included a stopover at the Playboy mansion in Chicago in 1975, which this drawing may, or may not, be alluding to.

"He sold out years ago."

A couple of overdressed punks disparage Bob Dylan in 1978. Cartoonist Michael Heath was well known for his 'Tribes of Britain' feature in *Punch* magazine as well as 'Great Bores of Today' in *Private Eye*. He took great pleasure in drawing modish sub-groups of the population – and the way that they dressed – in intricate and uncannily accurate detail, thereby rendering them ridiculous and very amusing.

The Prodigal Daughter

LEFT: The kidnapping of 19 year-old Patty Hearst, granddaughter of press magnate William Randolph Hearst, sent shockwaves through America – these reached fever pitch when it transpired that Hearst had allegedly participated in the illegal activities of her captors.

BELOW: Following Strategic Arms Limitation Talks (SALT II) in Vienna in 1979, Brezhnev and Carter came to an agreement on warheads and launcher systems, but it couldn't be ratified after the Soviets invaded Afghanistan in 1980. (by John Jensen)

In 1977 Mel Brooks released *High Anxiety* which is a tribute of sorts to Alfred Hitchcock and his suspense films *Spellbound*, *Vertigo* and *The Birds*. Hitchcock helped Brooks to work up the screenplay and later sent him six magnums of 1961 Château Haut-Brion, a classic Bordeaux

OPPOSITE: Idi Amin, President of Uganda, loved to award himself medals and titles. He was His Excellency President for Life, Field Marshal Al Hadji Doctor, the Uncrowned King of Scotland, Idi Amin VC DSO MC and Conqueror of the British Empire. He was also one of the 20th century's worst tyrants, responsible for 500,000 deaths by the time he was exiled in 1979. Valtman portrays a watchful, bloated figure with a very small head.

"I DON'T THINK WE'RE GONNA MAKE IT ANOTHER FOUR"

©1985 HERBLOCK

Parodying Grant Wood's *American Gothic*, Herb Block suggests that President Reagan
betrayed the farmers who voted him into the White House for a second term in 1985.

1980s

'Greed is good,' proclaimed Gordon Gekko in the film *Wall Street* and the 1980s was a period of laissez-faire capitalism. The decade saw a steady drift towards the right as the Soviet empire began to teeter, with Gorbachev becoming leader of the USSR in 1985, the overthrow of several regimes in eastern Europe and the fall of the Berlin wall. Elsewhere, there was the invasion of Grenada, civil war in El Salvador, the Battle for the Falklands and John Lennon was shot dead outside his home in New York. The DeLorean car was introduced, the internet developed and MTV was launched, making huge stars of many new artists. In fashion, this was the decade of big hair, shoulder pads and New Romantics.

'WE WANT THE OLYMPICS TO BE A PURE SPORTING EVENT – NOT AN OPPORTUNITY FOR THE WESTERN NEWS MEDIA TO LIONIZE DISSIDENTS AND TO PLAY POLITICS'

Ed Valtman depicts Russian nuclear physicist and Nobel Peace Prize winner Andrei Sakharov being led away in handcuffs made up of the Olympic rings, while Soviet leader Leonid Brezhnev defends his detention. Sakharov was arrested in January 1980 following his public criticism of the Soviet invasion of Afghanistan in December. America initiated a boycott of the Moscow Olympics that summer in response to the invasion. Around 50 countries pulled out.

"Say . . . You're beautiful when you're angry."

A *Punch* cartoon from 1982, commenting on the 'special relationship' between President Reagan and British Prime Minister Margaret Thatcher. Cold War tensions resurfaced in the early 1980s following the détente of the 1970s. Thatcher shoots at a target in the shape of Soviet leader Yuri Andropov, egged on by Reagan who paraphrases a John Wayne quote – a nod to his own Hollywood background and the gung-ho approach of the 1950s Western.

'Trog' (Wally Fawkes) presents the Prince of Pop Art, Andy Warhol, in this *Punch* cartoon from 1986. Warhol remained at the heart of the artistic scene in New York throughout the 1980s, striking up friendships with a number of its rising stars, such as Jean-Michel Basquiat and Julian Schnabel. From the early 1980s, he also pioneered the use of new, computer-generated art software. Warhol died following routine surgery in 1987.

"AND NOW SOME MORE OFFICIAL INFORMATION ON THE ACCIDENT AT CHERNOBYL"

On 26 April 1986 a reactor exploded at the Chernobyl Nuclear Power Plant in the Ukraine, resulting in deaths, the resettlement of thousands of people and the contamination of millions of acres of land – the effects of the radiation were even felt as far away as North Wales. Herb Block depicts a skeletal family listening to the radio, alluding to the failure of the Soviet government to issue timely information about the extent of the disaster.

"OUR BAGS ARE PACKED"
— Weinberger on Star Wars program

©1987 HERBLOCK

Herb Block pulled no punches when attacking what he viewed as the dishonest and greedy Reagan administration. Here the target is Defense Secretary Caspar Weinberger, who pushed for increased arms spending and supported Reagan's delusional plans for a space-based, anti-missile programme, known as 'Star Wars'. The price-tag on the toilet seat refers to the disclosure that the Pentagon had, *inter alia*, spent $600 on ashtrays and $2,043 on wing nuts.

The publication of Salman Rushdie's *The Satanic Verses* in 1988 provoked protests across the Islamic world: in 1989 a *fatwa* was issued against the author by the Supreme Leader of Iran, Ayatollah Ruhollah Khomeini. Ed McLachlan's cartoon suggests substituting Rushdie with Jeffrey Archer, for his less illustrious contribution to the literary canon.

"The British still say the death sentence against Salman Rushdie is unacceptable - but would you consider Jeffrey Archer instead?"

Herb Block shows presidential candidate George H. W. Bush greeting potential voters in a diner in this cartoon from 1988. Bush suceeded Reagan in 1989, becoming the first Vice President to be elected President since 1836.

"Oh no!"

Prince Charles offered some outspoken views on architecture during the 1980s. In 1988, a year after this *Punch* cartoon was produced, he expressed his hatred of modern styles during a TV documentary, notably condemning Birmingham city centre as a 'monstrous concrete maze'. Here, David Langdon imagines the heir apparent's horror when Prince William displays a liking for Brutalist forms – as well as noting the tense relationship between Charles and Diana, who appears to be egging the young Prince on.

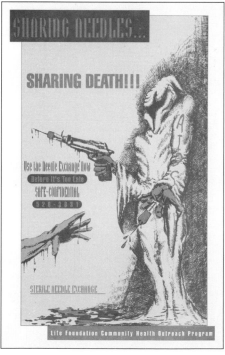

In 1985, actor Rock Hudson became the first American celebrity to publically annouce that he had AIDS. His death in October had an immediate impact on the visibility of the disease in American society, and on funding research into its cause. Posters such as this one for a needle exchange programme in Honolulu, Hawaii reflected the growing understanding and awareness of how AIDS could be transmitted.

Soviet leader Mikhail Gorbachev balances Humpty-Dumpty-like on top of a wall, representing the crumbling USSR. The Soviet Union was dissolved on 26 December 1991.

1990s

The final decade of the 20th century saw the release of Nelson Mandela after 27 years in jail, the first successful cloning of a mammal and the end of the Cold War. Wars broke out in Eastern European – Kosovo, Chechnya – and in the Middle East. After over a quarter of a century of conflict in Northern Ireland, the Good Friday Agreement marked a turning point towards peace. The World Wide Web went public in 1991 and Apple's iMac G3 launched a new age of internet computers seven years later. Sitcoms flooded TV screens and even made an impact in the hairdresser's (remember 'The Rachel'?). Although the world had changed a lot in 100 years, the work of political cartoonists could still pack a punch.

TURNING A BLIND EYE

In 1990 Margaret Thatcher's government introduced the unpopular Community Charge (or 'poll tax'). The tax was widely criticized, viewed as particularly unfair for people on lower incomes. There were a number of anti-poll tax demonstrations throughout the UK, the largest of which took place in Trafalgar Square on 31 March 1990. The fall-out from the poll tax ultimately led to the resignation of Thatcher eight months later.

Nicholas Garland's cartoon for *The Independent* marks the signing of the 'Groote Schuur Minute' between Nelson Mandela of the African National Congress and the President of South Africa, F. W. De Klerk, on 4 May 1990. The two parties agreed to end violence in South Africa and work towards peace. Mandela succeeded De Klerk as president in 1994.

"AND THEY SHALL BEAT THEIR SWORDS INTO PLOUGHSHARES..."

John Jensen for the *Mail on Sunday*. In September 1991 British Prime Minister John Major became the first leader of a Western European country to visit China in more than two years, following the massacre of civilians in Tiananmen Square in 1989. The areas of concern to the West are displayed on the Lazy Susan, including China's human rights record – hence a disdainful Major holding his nose with chopsticks.

Ed Valtman presents Marx, Lenin and Stalin looking down from their 'Communist Paradise' in dismay, as Soviet leader Mikhail Gorbachev leads a funeral procession for Communism. Gorbachev had notably transferred power from the Communist Party to elected representatives within the USSR's republics in 1990. Such developments, along with the fall of the Berlin Wall, signalled the end of the Cold War.

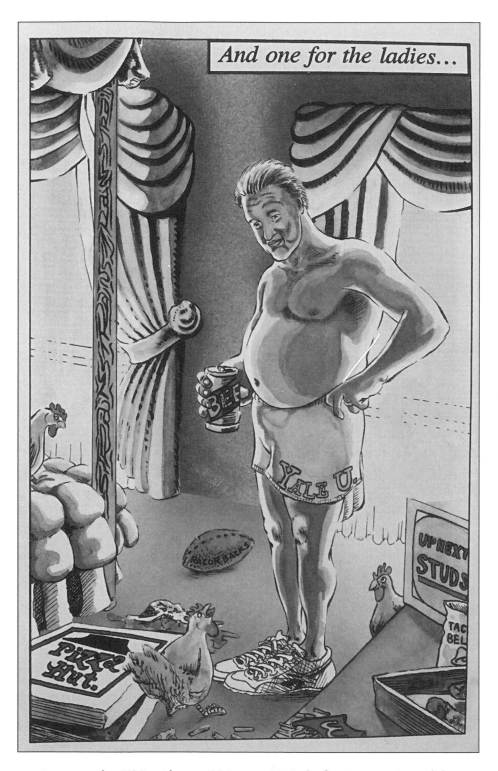

Bill Clinton was inaugurated as US President on 20 January 1993, the first Democratic candidate to win the White House since 1981. But his campaign was not without controversy – during the New Hampshire primary model and actress Gennifer Flowers claimed she'd had a 12-year affair with the sax-playing politician. This cartoon appeared in a comic book at the time, allegedly detailing events in the Clinton-Flowers relationship.

'Does anybody know if we're all here?'

A *Punch* cartoon referring to the Brooke-Mayhew talks between Northern Ireland political parties and British and Irish governments between 1991 and 1992. The 1990s saw significant developments in the Northern Ireland peace process. In 1994 the IRA declared a ceasefire and on 10 April 1998 the Good Friday Agreement was signed – its principal aims were to end violence and to establish new Irish political institutions.

This cartoon by Nicholas Garland appeared in *The Independent* on 1 November 1990 and shows American President George H. W. Bush embarking on a last-minute game of chess (in which the pieces are all missiles) with Iraqi President Saddam Hussein. By November 1990 the Gulf War, which had been sparked by Iraq's invasion of Kuwait, was entering its second month.

'I would have preferred the royal handshake': cartoon from a 1991 edition of *Punch*. The British monarchy came under increasing scrutiny and criticism during the 1990s, beginning with the government's announcement of reforms to the royal finances – in 1993 the Queen became the first British monarch to pay income tax since the 1930s. This cartoon by Martin Honeysett appears to show her headbutting MPs for considering the introduction of the new tax arrangements. But the antics of several family members and a number of acrimonious divorces continued to attract negative publicity. Public anger reached its peak following the premature death of Princess Diana in August 1997, when the Royals' initial response appeared cold and out of touch.

LINES IN THE SAND

Herb Block's response to the war in Kosovo (1998–1999) was published in the *Washington Post* on 26 February 1999. The cartoon shows how the then President of Yugoslavia, Slobodan Milosevic, was ignoring feeble NATO attempts to prevent Serbian forces from entering Kosovo. Milosevic was indicted for crimes against humanity and in 2006 died in his cell in The Hague while waiting for the verdict to be handed down.

"KIDS THESE DAYS! CRAZINESS IN SCHOOLS, MOVIES, VIDEO GAMES — TERRIBLE! HERE — TRY THIS LITTLE DANDY"

Herb Block produced this cartoon for the *Washington Post* on 28 April 1999, eight days after the Columbine High School massacre in Colorado, in which two teenagers shot and killed twelve of their fellow students and a teacher before committing suicide. The shooting lead to an increased focus on security in US schools and prompted debates over gun control laws and the influence of violent films and video games in American society.

'Damn. They've seen us'

Some of the most significant social and cultural developments of the 1990s were aided by the creation of new technologies, such as cable television and the internet. Tim Berners-Lee's World Wide Web became publically accessible in 1991; by 1999 almost every country in the world had a connection. With ever-increasing demand for programming, there are now very few regions of the world that have not been extensively visited for documentaries. Even penguins at the South Pole are media-savvy in this cartoon by Tony Husband from 1991.

Picture Credits

With particular thanks to the following people for their help and assistance: Claire Colvin, Jeffrey Frith, Andre Gailani, Nicholas Garland and John Jensen.

We have made every effort to contact the copyright holders of the images used in this book. In a few cases, we have been unable to do so, but we will be very happy to credit them in future editions.

Alexander Turnbull Library, Wellington, New Zealand: 118

The Bridgeman Art Library: 18 (Bibliotheque Nationale, Paris/Archives Charmet), 90 (Brooklyn Museum of Art, New York/Gift of Spencer Bickerton)

Clifford H. Baldowski Editorial Cartoon Collection, Richard B. Russell Library for Political Research and Studies, University of Georgia Libraries, Athens: 155

Sam Cobean/The New Yorker Collection/The Cartoon Bank: 129

Corbis: 12 (Bettman), 15 (Bettman), 20 (Bettman), 31 (Heritage Images), 39 (Bettman), 42b (Bettman), 55 (Underwood & Underwood), 72 (Bettman), 97t (Bettman), 99, 125 (Bettman), 130, 142t, 152b (Michael Nicholson), 159t (Bettman), 168

Neville Colvin: 144t

John Frith: 154t

Nicholas Garland: 195t, 199t, 203 (all supplied by the British Cartoon Archive, University of Kent)

Getty Images: 24t, 56, 75 (UIG), 83, 88, 92 (UIG), 94, 95, 157 (Time & Life Pictures), 201

The Herblock Foundation: 101, 115, 126, 132, 150, 156, 162, 172, 174, 186, 191, 192, 193b, 205, 206

Rea Irvin/The New Yorker Collection/The Cartoon Bank: 79t

John Jensen: 154b, 176 (both supplied by the British Cartoon Archive, University of Kent), 183b, 199b

Library Archives Canada: 119tl

Mary Evans Picture Library: 38 (Everett Collection), 49, 76-77 (Everett Collection)

Ohio State University Library and Special Collections: 105

Reproduced with permission of Punch Limited (www.punch.co.uk): 19, 30t, 34, 43, 50, 54, 68, 69, 70, 71, 78, 82, 93, 96, 100, 102, 106, 123, 124, 134, 135, 137, 139, 141, 142b, 143, 144b, 146, 149, 151t, 159b, 160t, 160b, 163b, 164t, 165, 166-167, 170, 171, 179t, 180, 181, 182, 185, 189, 190, 193t, 194, 196, 198, 202, 204, 207

Solo Syndication/Associated Newspapers Ltd: 122, 136, 151b (all supplied by the British Cartoon Archive, University of Kent)

Topfoto: 10-11 (Fine Art Images/Heritage Images), 14 (The Granger Collection), 21 (The Granger Collection), 22, 24b (The Granger Collection), 25 (World History Archive), 26 (World History Archive), 27 (The Granger Collection), 35, 36t (The Granger Collection), 37, 40 (World History Archive), 41 (The Granger Collection), 44 (The Granger Collection), 46, 47t (The Granger Collection), 47b, 52 (ullsteinbild), 53 (The Granger Collection), 57 (The Granger Collection), 62 (The Granger Collection), 66 (The Granger Collection), 67 (The Granger Collection), 73 (The Granger Collection), 74 (The Granger Collection), 79b (Print Collector/HIP), 81 (The Granger Collection), 84 (The Granger Collection), 85 (The Granger Collection), 86 (The Granger Collection), 89 (The Granger Collection), 91t (The Granger Collection), 98, 103 (The Granger Collection), 108, 109, 112, 114 (The Granger Collection), 116 (The Granger Collection), 117 (The Granger Collection), 120 (The Granger Collection), 121 (The Granger Collection), 127t, 128 (The Granger Collection), 133 (The Granger Collection), 138 (The Granger Collection), 140 (The Granger Collection), 145 (The Granger Collection), 153b, 158 (World History Archive), 175 (Fine Art Images/Heritage Images)

US Library of Congress: 8, 9, 16-17, 23t, 28-29, 51t, 61, 148, 153t, 161, 173, 177, 178, 179b, 186, 188, 200

Wellcome Collection Images: 23b, 127b, 195b